SET FREE TO LOVE

SET FREE TO LOVE

LIVES
CHANGED
by the
THEOLOGY
of the
BODY

Marcel LeJeune

SERVANT
BOOKS

PUBLISHED BY ST. ANTHONY MESSENGER PRESS
CINCINNATI, OHIO

Scripture passages have been taken from the *Revised Standard Version*, Catholic edition. Copyright 1946, 1952, 1971 by the Division of Christian Education of the National Council of Churches of Christ in the USA. Used by permission. All rights reserved.

Cover design by Candle Light Studios
Cover image copyright © Maciej Noskowski photography
Book design by Mark Sullivan

LIBRARY OF CONGRESS CATALOGING-IN-PUBLICATION DATA
Set free to love : lives changed by the theology of the body / [edited by] Marcel LeJeune.
p. cm.
Includes bibliographical references (p.   ) and index.
ISBN 978-0-86716-940-9 (pbk. : alk. paper) 1. Human body—Religious aspects—Catholic Church. 2. John Paul II, Pope, 1920-2005. Theology of the body. 3. John Paul II, Pope, 1920-2005. 4. Sex—Religious aspects—Catholic Church. 5. Catholic Church—Doctrines. I. LeJeune, Marcel.
BX1795.B63S48 2010
233'.5—dc22

2010028384

ISBN 978-0-86716-940-9

Published by Servant Books, an imprint of St. Anthony Messenger Press.
28 W. Liberty St.
Cincinnati, OH 45202
www.AmericanCatholic.org
www.ServantBooks.org

Printed in the United States of America.
Printed on acid-free paper.
10 11 12 13 14   5 4 3 2 1

ACKNOWLEDGMENTS

To our Trinitarian God, who made us
out of love, for love.

To Mary, our mother.

To John Paul the Great for his theology of the body.

To my wife and children, who are pure gifts to me.

To the contributors to this book.
Your stories inspire me and others.
Thank you for giving of yourselves as
gifts for the glory of God.

To all who worked on the editing of this book,
especially Cindy Cavnar.

To Servant Books and all who work to get the
Good News into print.

What Is the Theology of the Body?

The most common way of answering this question starts with the origin of the teaching—almost five years' worth of Wednesday audiences of Pope John Paul II, from 1979 to 1984, on the Trinitarian nature of God and our creation in the image and likeness of the Trinity as bodily creatures. This truth is in no way limited to the Wednesday addresses but is present in the entire body of John Paul II's writings, both before and after he was chosen as pope.

Another good answer to the question "What is the theology of the body?" lies in the topics covered—sex, chastity, married life, celibacy, Trinitarian love, human dignity, the differences between men and women, and our ultimate purpose in life.

Both approaches answer the question in different ways. But from my perspective, the theology of the body is more than either of these definitions: It is a life-changing tool. It changed my life, as it has countless other lives.

I was first introduced to the theology of the body in graduate school in the year 2000. The teaching does not come easily to most people, and this was the case for me as well. I had to learn the language that John Paul II used in what is called his phenomenological approach—that is, a philosophy based upon human experiences. Also, John Paul II has a "spiral" approach to teaching this subject matter: He revisits topics from another perspective, looking at them in new ways that build upon what he has previously taught. The teaching is dense, leading many people who try to study it to give up.

Yet I can assure you it is worth the effort it takes to comprehend this teaching. More than anything else I studied while in graduate school, the theology of the body was intellectual candy for me. It gave me insights into God and my own life that were truly exciting.

Coming to understand the basics of John Paul II's teaching is one thing, but absorbing it deeply is another. I recognized in the teaching a call to conversion, and like every call to conversion, there are only two responses, yes and no.

In the Beginning

Karol Wojtyla was a man who bore some heavy crosses. His only sister died before he was born, his mother died when he was a child, and his only brother died when Karol was just thirteen. Raised by his father, Karol dove into acting and his academic studies. Through it all he maintained a deep prayer life, and in that prayer he discerned a call to the priesthood.

Karol's pursuit of the priesthood was interrupted by World War II and the consequent invasion of his homeland, Poland. Forced to study in an underground seminary because of Nazi restrictions on the Church, Karol learned what kind of evil man is capable of. He learned this lesson once again when the Communists continued to suppress the Church after the war and to sponsor various atrocities against human life and liberty.

The theology of the body is a response to the false philosophies of the human person that come from fascism, communism, materialism, nihilism, Manichaeism, dualism, and other misguided theories. These philosophies all fail to understand the worth of every human being and the origin of that worth. The truth of the theology of the body not only transcends these false philosophies but also gives us the antidote to the evils that plague us today.

As a young parish pastor, Fr. Karol became friends with many young people—singles and married couples, some with children. Their experiences of life and human relationships prompted him to meditation and study of the truth about humanity and our nature, particularly our creation in the divine image. Years of study led him to begin a manuscript that he intended to publish, but before he could complete it, he was elected pope. He decided to make his findings the heart of the pontifical teaching he would give the Church.

The theology of the body starts with a novel approach to the first few chapters of Genesis in light of the teachings of Christ. In this examination John Paul II focuses his attention on man's creation and who man was before, during, and after the Fall, as well as humanity's ultimate destiny, heaven. Throughout this teaching the pope builds a new Christian anthropology (a teaching about humanity) as well as a deeper understanding of theology (a teaching about the nature of God).

I knew the story of creation well. I had read and heard it dozens of times, as most of us have. But I had never truly seen it with the depth that John Paul II provides. When I first studied the theology of the body, I felt as if I were reading the book of Genesis for the first time, because it came alive through the pope's insights. I love "lightbulb moments" (think of the cartoon characters having a lightbulb go off when they get a good idea), and the theology of the body provided a number of them for me, so I thoroughly enjoyed studying it.

The pope begins his focus on humanity's relationship with God by considering the relationship of God with Adam and Eve. Adam, the prototypical man, is created in communion with God. He walks and talks with God in the Garden of Eden. John Paul II refers to this as man's "original solitude."

Yet Adam does not feel complete. His deepest longings are not fully met. In Genesis 2:18 God says, "It is not good that the man should be alone." In creating humanity God put a deep longing within for communion with others, both God and other humans. This longing is not met by the other parts of creation with which God surrounds Adam—an indication that man is called to something higher than the rest of creation.

Most of us have experienced the longing for God in the restlessness of life, a longing that will never be fully satisfied this side of heaven. St. Augustine's famous line speaks to the universal experience of this desire: "You have made us for yourself, O Lord, and our hearts are restless until they rest in you."[1]

Yet there is also that desire for human companionship. Thus the Father creates Eve. In her Adam finds fulfillment of his longing for another: "This at last is bone of my bones and flesh of my flesh" (Genesis 2:23).

This raises a question: How does communion between humans fulfill a desire for communion with God?

The body, John Paul II teaches, is made to reflect the communion with God for which we are created. Male and female bodies are created to be together in the sexual act as husband and wife, and our souls are made to complement each other in a spiritual communion. There is a built-in complementarity that God intends, and in this complementarity—in our maleness and femaleness coming together—we find a sacramental reflection of the divine. In our sexuality (being made male and female) and in the mystery of marriage, we find the answers to our deepest questions about ourselves.

This view of human love as a reflection of divine love opened up a whole new world for me. It gave me a deeper understanding of the love God has for me, for others, and for the whole of creation. I could also see clearly that I was called to love others. The value of my being, including the sacred importance of the body, was exposed to me as never before.

John Paul II teaches that, "the body, and it alone, is capable of making visible what is invisible."[2] The body, in the sexual union of husband and wife, shows the inner working of God in the Trinity. This happens because marital love was intentionally created to reflect the divine love of God.

Within the Trinity the Father always, and for all time, has given himself as a gift to his Son, the Second Person of the Trinity. This gift of love is received by the Son and returned, in full, to the Father. In this giving and receiving we find the definition of love—gift. This gift of self that we call love is, in fact, the Holy Spirit. The Third Person of the Trinity proceeds from the love between the Father and the Son: He is love itself. Hence 1 John 4:8 says, "God is love."

Married couples echo this Trinitarian love in what Genesis 2:24 calls the "one flesh" union of our sexuality. The male body is designed to be the giver and the female to be the receiver of the man's gift. The woman reciprocates by giving herself to the man, and he receives her fully.

This gift of love between man and woman is embodied in their children. Just as the love of the Father and the Son is personified through the Holy Spirit, the love of a husband and wife is personified in their children. Thus the love between man and woman becomes a reflection of the divine love of God and raises our sexuality to what it was supposed to be "in the beginning."

Furthermore, we are called to live out this love by being gifts to others in everything we do. We are created to give ourselves away to our families, our friends, and everyone else we encounter. Ultimately the entire gift of our selves is given to God, who is the supreme giver of the Gift, Jesus.

In the Present

Humanity was originally made in this taste of divine love. But even with Eve, the one who fulfills Adam's longing for communion, the unity of spouses doesn't last long. Adam and Eve eat the apple. We all suffer the consequences and share in their original sin. Life is not a Garden of Eden anymore.

Before the Fall no shame or lust resulted from Adam and Eve's nakedness. But once they sinned, shame and lust entered in. So the two clothed themselves, sewing fig leaves together because they lusted for one another.

Shame is a natural protector from lust; it is a necessity in our fallen world. But shame scars our relationships, and the battle between real love and lust still rages in our hearts. Our sinful nature leads us to want to use others, which John Paul II says is the opposite of true love. We have a sinful tendency to grasp and take, which is contrary to what will fulfill our desire to give and receive love. We all experience this tug in our relationships, and we have to fight the tendency to use other people.

But we can recapture the original relationship with God

and others, if not in whole on this earth. This is the case only because Jesus became a gift for us. The Bible tells us in Ephesians 5:31–32 that we are the spouse Christ has come to marry. In this marriage of divine and human, we are called to live out the experience of communion.

John Paul II provides a new understanding of the hope of Christ's redemption of our bodies and our sexuality. God didn't leave us to suffer needlessly in our pride, lust, sin, and death. Rather he calls us to find, in relationship with him, redemption of our bodies and renewal of true love, which is the gift of self to both God and other human beings. Capturing and living out this radical view of the nature of humanity is life altering.

God created humans to live with him forever in heaven. This is the ultimate marriage each of us looks forward to. We are all espoused to God if we choose to accept the gift of the Son. Yet God will never force himself on any of us, because he is a gentle lover. He will woo us and call to us but never coerce. It is always our choice, made in freedom, to love God.

Our bodies reflect this future reality in the present but in different ways, through different vocations. Some are called to be single, others to marry, still others to be religious or priests. Yet all of us are called to chastity, that is, the proper ordering of our sexuality in whatever state of life we are.

Chastity is the virtue that sets love free from the slavery of our sexual passions. Chastity does not take away our freedom but rather sets us free to love others. In fact, if we fail to become chaste, we can never truly love another person, and thus we can never truly and deeply love God.

All of us are single for a portion of our lives, and in the unmarried state of life we are called to chaste celibacy. This isn't a no to sex but rather a yes to divine love and love of others as humans, not using them as objects for our selfish pleasure. In a more extraordinary way, the celibacy of the priesthood and religious life is a permanent yes to the marriage that we will all have with God in heaven. This is exactly what Christ meant when he said that some are called to give up earthly marriage "for the sake of the kingdom" (Matthew 19:12).

The vocation of earthly marriage also foreshadows the heavenly marriage and, like the priesthood, does so in a sacramental way. Marriage is a sign, or sacrament, of what will happen in heaven. Through the sexual act of husband and wife, the bodies of two reflect the spiritual marriage of Christ and all of us, his Church.

In My Life

My study of the theology of the body was challenging. I learned about God, life, myself, sexuality (being made male and female), and human dignity. But I had to *do* something about it in order to move it from my head to my heart.

This theology of the body has ramifications for every part of the Christian life. My own reflection on it brought many questions to the surface:

- If sex is meant to be something great—a reflection of God himself—then how do I order my sex life?
- If my body isn't just about pleasure but is integral to who I am as a human, how do I order my sexuality toward the love and worship of God?
- Is my life a gift to my wife, my family, my friends, and others?
- If sex is great, beautiful, and wonderful, how can I redeem the false sense I have that it is dirty, bad, and ugly?
- Am I reflecting God's love through my body?

By the time I was studying this profound teaching, I was already married and had a child. It was during this time that I decided to put the theology of the body to a thirty-day test. If this teaching really was as revolutionary as I thought it was, then it would have to change me.

I grew up with an intense hatred for doing the dishes. This was not just the standard "why do I have to?" attitude but a stubborn disdain for the task. There were seven of us in my family, and we dirtied a lot of dishes. From an early age it was my job to wash them. In my juvenile selfishness I wanted to be served; I didn't want to serve others. Thus, washing the dishes became the chore I despised.

I tried every tactic I could think of to get out of washing the dishes. I would procrastinate until threats of more chores came from my mother. I would make excuses. I would even lie to try to get out of them. Once I eventually got around to washing the dishes, I was in for additional work, because by then the food would have become hard and dry.

Now, we did have a dishwasher, but it was not a very good one. So my mother would constantly check to make sure I prewashed all of the dishes before running the machine. Mom wasn't afraid to make me wash dishes twice if I didn't get the job right the first time.

When I went away to college, I never gave dishes a second thought, because I ate most meals in restaurants or in the dorm cafeteria. I came to believe that the dish carousel in the cafeteria was a magical machine that solved my dishes problem. After I got married, however, the dishes came back into my life, as did my negative attitude. I took every chance I could to get out of doing them, just as I had done as a child. My wife and I had arguments about the dishes similar to arguments heard in millions of households around the globe.

"Honey, can you help with the dishes tonight?"

"But I did them last night!"

"Yes, but I emptied the trash and vacuumed."

"That is nothing. I mowed the lawn."

"*Fine!* I'll do them, but you owe me!"

I certainly was keeping score and using my wife as my personal maid. One day it dawned on me, through the grace of God, that my anti-dishwashing attitude was a failure on my part to love my wife and to see her as God's gift to me. So I decided from that day forward to make doing the dishes my desire.

During my thirty-day theology of the body challenge, I didn't immediately enjoy doing the dishes, but my perspective gradually changed. Instead of trying to get out of a hated duty, I saw the dishes as a chance to love my wife—to die to my own desires and be a true gift to her. I could choose what was best for her regardless of what it cost me.

Underlying this attitude change was a paradigm shift at a deeper level. I looked at my heart and realized that I wasn't in relationships, including my marriage, in order to give myself away in love but rather to get the most for myself. This is the definition of selfishness, but I hadn't even seen it. Instead of sacrificing myself for my wife, my children, my extended family, my friends, and others, I was trying to use them.

Pope John Paul II teaches in his theology of the body that using another person as a means to an end is the opposite of true love. True love, according to the pope, is giving your entire self to others and loving them as an end in itself. My head realized what I was doing; then my heart started to change, as well as my actions. In no way have I reached perfection in this love, but my mind and heart are properly oriented now, so I have the opportunity to love more humbly, selflessly, fully, and fruitfully.

At the end of the thirty days, my wife and I were lying in bed with the lights out, talking. I asked how she thought our marriage was going. She told me that it had never been better. It was then that I let her in on my secret thirty-day theology of the body challenge. She was flabbergasted, to say the least.

Our marriage has never been the same. Since that day, over eight years ago, we have never fought about chores around the house—that is, unless she has tried to do the dishes herself.

In the Future

The changes in my life didn't stop with the dishes. I also started to see the world in a new way. Not only did God create us good, not only are our bodies and souls to be perfectly integrated, but we are also called to see God's goodness in all of the created order.

I had absorbed many lies about the body in my mind and actions. (The culture certainly is no ally in helping us see the truth about our bodies.) One lie is the worship of the body and sex. This philosophy tells us happiness comes from bodily pleasure seeking, wherever we may find it. We find evidence of such trappings in our modern advertisements, which tell us to use their products and become irresistible to the opposite sex. Once we are able to have pleasure, they say, then happiness and fulfillment are sure to follow.

Another lie is that we are merely spirits trapped in bodies, which we must escape in order to find what it means to be human. This pseudo-mystical approach to the human body is a dualistic understanding of the human person. The body is the raw material, this idea goes, and the mind and spirit use it for their own purposes. This is a disintegration, not a discovery, of what it means to be human.

The theology of the body stands as a contradiction to these modern philosophies about the body. It teaches that for us to truly understand our humanity, we must embrace our bodies and the goodness in them, not reject them or worship them. Our bodies are not bad, nor are they just good. They are for a sacred purpose. They are also integral to our identity as humans.

I have been blessed to see and hear about many lives changed by John Paul's theology of the body, and I believe we need this teaching more with every passing year. The rapid changes in our culture have created an environment in which it is difficult for many to see the truth about humans and God. Many modern ears are deaf to the gospel. We need a new approach to spreading the Good News of Jesus Christ. I believe the theology of the body gives us a great tool to do this.

To be good evangelists, we must first overcome the numerous deceptions in our modern culture. The Catholic Church is nearly alone in standing against many of these deceptions, including that of "sexual equality." Do I mean that the Church must view women and men as unequal? Not at all! Indeed, the Church views male and female as equal but not in the narrow sense that society does.

Modern society has a litmus test for human value and human relationships: This test is basically one of function. In a function-based equality, the roles that women once had are now open for men to fulfill, and vice versa. We all are capable of "doing what everyone else does," regardless of our nature. This justifies the idea of having women priests, because women can proclaim the gospel, wear vestments, give homilies, run parishes, and so on. People can "marry" someone of the same sex, because all function the same in such "marriages."

This way of thinking about humanity is a denial of the purpose for which God created us male and female. Thinking we can be whatever we want, just by willing it, boils down to a refutation of what God intends each of us to be. Attempting to make men and women equal ends up making them the same, thus denying precisely that which truly makes us equal: our reflection of the divine.

People who approach human interaction this way tend to conclude that the Church is archaic and sexist. But in the eyes of the Church, equality between men and women is based on something much more important than mere function.

An important note we must make about the creation narrative we explored previously is that Adam was not referred to as "male" until there was a female to contrast with his maleness. John Paul II teaches that, prior to Eve, Adam is just "man," as in mankind as a whole, with no consideration of sexuality. Adam only takes on the masculinity that is part of his nature after Eve is created. She provides the femininity that gives masculinity its meaning. In other words, without female there is no male. God created this distinction between male and female.

Once Eve is created we have not only man and woman but also husband and wife. The two become one. They complement each other in the differences that they bear by their nature. But the two are not interchangeable. The woman cannot be husband, and the man cannot be wife. *In their differences they find what the other needs to be complete.*

Thus the Church has a view that is in conflict with society's view of sexuality, the meaning of the human person, the body, and God. True equality can only be found by acknowledging our differences and then finding that which transcends them. Our dignity is tied to the relationship that God created between men and women at the beginning.

This teaching on the equality of men and women, which Pope John Paul II has refined most recently, allows a new approach to the age-old problem of defending the Church's teaching on many topics. We can now delve into the meaning of sexuality, relationships, and the dignity of humanity. We discover that God really does know what he is doing when he teaches us about gender and human worth.

It isn't just a matter of knowing the truths of the Church; it is also important to order our lives to the will of God and how he sees the world. We are men and women created in the image of God. We are children of a loving Father. We reflect his image back to him and the world. This is what we are about.

In the New Beginning

This might be your first introduction to the theology of the body, or you may know something about it already. Regardless of your level of knowledge, I ask you to enter into this book with an open heart, ready to see how God wants to change your life. Each one of the stories that follows has one purpose: to help you hear the call to live out the gift of love in your own life, in your own way, however God may call you to do it.

The stories come from people from all walks of life—single, married, priest, and religious. The stories differ but share one common thread: God works through the teachings found in the theology of the body to change hearts and lives.

You cannot love what you do not know, and so I ask you to study the theology of the body—not for the sake of merely gaining knowledge but for the sake of conforming your life to the mission and identity of Christ himself. I have included a list of helpful resources in the back of this book. Through learning who God is, who we are, and what our ultimate purpose is in life, may we all choose redemption, transformation, and conversion. This is what it means to live the theology of the body.

FRENCH BISQUE WITH BODY
Fr. Benjamin P. Bradshaw

Anyone who has lived through a crisis situation—an auto accident, the horror of war, or some other trauma—knows that the mind might simply shut out what is actually happening or even shut down as a means of self-protection. Some people experience Posttraumatic Stress Syndrome years after a particularly tragic event. Put simply, the occurrence is too painful to grasp. Often people will say, "It happened in slow motion."

Similarly, there are times when we experience a joy so vast and profound that the mind cannot expand enough to take it in. Likewise it is often as if "it happened in slow motion." I found just such a joy through the theology of the body.

The Italian Desert

In October of 1998 I was living on the Adriatic side of central Italy with a Catholic religious community, discerning my vocation to the priesthood. I had worked as a missionary with this community in Russia three years prior and had decided to spend a year in prayer, trying to figure out what God was calling me to do in my life.

I had spent my adult years as a professional chef, obtaining culinary degrees and working with some of the most demanding chefs Memphis, Tennessee, had to offer. But then God happened. I felt a pull to go deeper and, quite possibly, into a vocation to the Catholic priesthood.

Quite frankly, it had not been going well. My personal prayer was as dry as the Sahara Desert: God seemed completely absent. Inwardly I was at a point of total desperation. Here I was on the other side of the world, willing to give my life to God, and yet every time I sat down to pray and hear his voice, the only thing I heard was the sickening sound of silence, the echo of nothingness, and the absence of a God who seemed to be the author of some sick joke called "vocational discernment." I was lost, having a spiritual "freak-out" with a God who appeared to be, at best, completely apathetic to my discernment woes.

On the morning of October 11, 1998, I was in the community kitchen preparing a ginger-carrot bisque and sipping a cup of strong Lavazza coffee. Having attended three different cooking schools prior to the seminary, I had decided to share with the community the only thing I knew how to do, namely cook and eat, especially since it was apparent that my prayer was not working.

While I was cooking, my friend Joe, who is now a priest of the same community, rushed into the kitchen and said, "Let's go to Rome; there is something you will want to see."

"What is it?" I asked, a little annoyed, as my ginger-carrot bisque was on the verge of perfection.

"You'll see; just get in the van."

And so I went, deeply irritated now at not having yet added the heavy whipping cream and whole butter to the beautiful silken soup.

We drove the three hours to Rome, our vehicle weaving in and out of traffic like an X-wing fighter, coming close to being airborne more than once. We arrived at St. Peter's Square in Vatican City, and our driver, by some unknown miracle, found a parking space next to the Via con della Conciliazione, or the Road of the Conciliation as it is known, giving us a thirty-second walk to St. Peter's. There were chairs and Swiss Guards everywhere, and it was obvious that we would be having a Mass with the pope. Possibly a canonization?

It was an absolutely beautiful day, and by now I was over my irritation, finally finding peace with the fact that few people actually understand the complex beauties of a perfectly prepared French bisque. I followed the crowd of seminarians and priests as we continued to weave in and out of checkpoints, metal detectors, folding chairs, and tourists with cameras. I was getting tired, but since I was only a third of the age of some of the priests who were now nearly running, I figured I should just keep my mouth shut and continue following.

St. Peter and Esther

We made our way as far toward the altar set up outside of St. Peter's as we could. We sacrificed closer seats in order to get some located strategically on the aisle, so as to better see "the Man," Pope John Paul II.

After half an hour, and having regained my composure, I turned to Joe and asked, "OK, what's going on? Why are we here?"

He looked at me and smiled and said simply, "Today Esther gets her due!"

Perplexed, I asked, "What do you mean? Who is Esther?" But by now the music had started, the square was overflowing, and the pope was making his way out of St. Peter's.

As long as I had waited to see the pope, it was an electrifying moment. I almost didn't think it would really happen. But when it did, it happened, as is said, "in slow motion," and I strove to take it all in.

In retrospect I find it ironic that as I stood in the presence of the successor to the apostle Peter, and quite possibly only the third pope to be named one day "the Great," I found myself staring not at him but at a massive tapestry hanging from the central loggia overlooking St. Peter's. The Carmelite face on the cloth was one I knew quite well. It was the face of someone I had read about over the course of the years, a face that invited a thirst for truth: Edith Stein, or Sr. Teresa Benedicta a Cruce.

I had read plenty about this woman's life and had fallen in love with her heroic story. She was gassed at Auschwitz, with her sister Rosa and seven hundred other Catholics, Jews, and gypsies from Holland, in August of 1942. I marveled at her courageous defense of the dignity of women in light of the gospel, in a culture that often ignored it.

I stood in shock. This tough Jewish convert to Catholicism was being canonized on a beautiful Roman day, and there I was, in full view of "the Man" and the image of Edith, a modern-day Esther. I began jumping up and down like a schoolboy on Christmas morning, apparently enough to spur the Swiss Guard into giving me some surly looks and a seminarian to tell me to "cool it!"

Lo and behold, the reading was from the book of Esther, a courageous heroine who risked all for her people. John Paul II beautifully accentuated Sr. Teresa's acceptance of the cross of martyrdom and her selfless gift of her life for the Church, speaking truth to the power of the Nazi regime.

I stood without words, thinking of the poignant scene in John's Gospel when Pontius Pilate asks Jesus face-to-face, "What is truth?" (John 18:38). Mankind has either been running from this question or running to it for the last two thousand years. Here was a woman so immersed in its goodness that, as the Zyklon B gas filled her lungs, she slept in peace, knowing that she died on the side of truth and on the side of selfless love. Hers was a total and sincere gift of self.

Study of the Gift

Years later in the seminary, I wrote my master's thesis on St. Edith Stein's understanding of Christian femininity and its impact on Pope John Paul II's teachings on the feminine genius. Over the course of five years, I spent what seems like hundreds of nights tucked away in the seminary library on the basement floor, poring over documents such as *Mulieris Dignitatem, Familiaris Consortio*, and Edith's *The Science of the Cross*. I lived on Diet Coke, gummy bears, and good bibliographies. More than once I fell asleep in the basement and had to use my cell phone to call someone to let me out, much to their 2:00 AM annoyance.

During the course of our training, the seminarians were each issued an unblemished copy of John Paul's *Theology of the Body*. Back in my room I threw mine in the stack with Aristotle's *Nicomachean Ethics* and the *Commentary on the Code of Canon Law*, to be read at a much later date, preferably postretirement.

About a week later I was in the library basement again, reading Edith's writings on the dignity and vocation of women, and I saw something that made me stop and pause. I went back and reread it again, then again. Stein noted that a woman, by her nature, is fundamentally other-oriented, and within her soul has the capacity of empathy in sharing the cross of others and becoming a gift for them. This sounded deeply familiar. I turned to my copy of *The Sixteen Documents of Vatican II* and found number 24 of *Gaudium et Spes*, the Pastoral Constitution on the Church in the Modern World. It read: "Man cannot fully find himself, except through a sincere gift of himself to the other."

I was shocked. I read the Vatican II quote again and again. Edith had anticipated the council's proclamation—long before the Fathers ever had a crack at it—following our Lord's famous exhortation: "Greater love has no man than this, that a man lay down his life for his friends" (John 15:13).

As I continued to read and study, the pieces began to fall into place even more. I looked up and down the deserted library aisle, taking deep breaths of the musty scent of ancient theology books. I stood up and began pacing, talking to myself, convinced that I had either completely lost my sanity or was on a gummy-bear high.

I knew that John Paul II had made the same assertion regarding the dignity of women. I had read his Apostolic Letter on the Dignity of Women, published on the Feast of the Assumption in 1988, and it had moved me deeply. Likewise I had read his Letter to Women, written to the Beijing Conference on Women in 1995 and there delivered by the ever poised and articulate Mary Ann Glendon. It also had moved me. But there was something else, somewhere in his writings, that I had possibly read once in passing and had obviously forgotten.

I went to bed that night frustrated at my memory. It was as if I was trying to recall a name of an old friend at a party and ultimately yielding to senility.

From Death to Life

One week later the seminarians were given a weeklong furlough, and I went home to visit my parents. My mother was the only human being I knew who had actually read *The Theology of the Body* cover to cover, inserting thousands of side notes and cross-references. I had brought my fresh copy home, and I cunningly swapped it with my mother's. This would serve me well, as I would find that my instructors' questions in class were well anticipated within Mother's side notes.

About two months later I was in "the cave," my basement library retreat, doing research on Edith, when in a state of half slumber I stumbled upon John Paul II's teachings on the dignity of women within the theology of the body. My mother had written some brilliant notes, and my excitement built quickly while I continued to read. After two minutes I was hyperventilating. John Paul II's theology of the human body almost completely mirrored St. Edith's understanding of the sexual complementarity of men and women.

And there, in that musty cavern of centuries-old theology books, I came upon perhaps the most poignant theological insight that I had ever had: I am called to die! I realized, as the Second Vatican Council Fathers said, as St. Edith Stein had delineated, and as the pope had spent his life articulating, that we are each called to give our lives in service to and as gifts to another, what John Paul II describes as the nuptial meaning of the body. Just as the body reveals the person, and as our bodies were made to be gifts to others by marriage or celibate virginity, so am I called to die to myself and live now completely and forever for others.

For the first time in my life, I felt as if I might understand something about who and what God actually is, namely, a Gift of Self, the Word made flesh on a cross, calling us to follow him into eternity. And for the first time since October of 1998, I felt the soulful presence of a young priest from Krakow named

Karol and a Jewish convert with a brilliant smile. There in the library basement, surrounded by St. Augustine, St. Thomas Aquinas, and St. Edith Stein, I began to weep. Later I went to bed a happy man, having learned the essence of God and my eternal vocation.

....

Fr. Ben Bradshaw is a priest of the diocese of Memphis, Tennessee.

....

ONE FLESH
Mike and Chasity Short

Our story begins seven years ago. Newly married, we were attending a vibrant parish where, in passing, we heard about something called the theology of the body. At the time we didn't have any idea that this message would transform our lives forever.

A group called the Theology of the Body Evangelization Team (TOBET) was to give a talk for the singles of our parish. Curious but afraid of being kicked out, we hid our wedding rings, snuck in, and quietly sat at the back of the room. The talk was about the meaning of our bodies and how we were made in the image and likeness of the Most Holy Trinity.

We soon recognized that this message held the key to happiness in our marriage and healing from our past, though we had countless questions and doubts swirling in our minds. Over the next few months, we read and learned all we could on the subject. We met a married couple who were part of TOBET and began a friendship that was rooted in truth and honesty about some of life's most difficult questions.

Despite all the information we were gaining, it took time for the truths of the theology of the body to take root in our lives. Our hearts were hardened. Throughout our young lives we had accepted the deception society upheld as truth and, quite frankly, had been content to live that way. It would take a lot of work and even more grace to open our hearts and minds to the beauty and truth God was now revealing to us. Ever patient, God slowly worked a miracle in our hearts and transformed our lives.

Woman and Man

Chasity: Coming from a past marred by a sexual assault as a young teenager, followed by years of hurt, misuse, mistrust, and promiscuity, I was in deep need of healing. I had a year of counseling in college, through which I learned the psychological side of my earlier behaviors. Though the counseling did help somewhat, I was left with a nagging sense of deep self-hatred; I could not forgive myself. I had only begun to face the demons from my past.

Needless to say, this was not good preparation for marriage. Although Mike and I loved one another deeply, and intellectually I knew that Mike would lay down his life for me, I held on to a mistrust of men that resulted from years of destructive behavior. I desperately wanted to give my whole self to Mike, but how could I, since I didn't have self-possession to begin with? Complete self-donation was not an option at this point, and so our marriage was not whole.

Mike and I lost our first child, Cullen, through miscarriage at three months. I saw this as yet another assault on my sexuality.

Mike: I had a typical upbringing for a boy during the late eighties and nineties. Television was laden with sexual references, and the Internet was available. I began masturbating at the age of eleven or twelve and promptly moved into an addiction to Internet pornography.

However, I thought of myself as a "good guy." I listened to my conscience enough to hold out on full-blown sexual intercourse, although everything else was fair game. I foolishly thought of myself as being on a kind of moral high ground because I was not "using" women by having sex with them and discarding them, as so many of my friends were. I was nice to girls and tried to be sensitive to their needs and was as faithful as a teenager could be.

That being said, my Internet pornography consumption was destroying me from the inside out. The "nice guy" image I portrayed belied a fantasy sex life that conditioned me to manipulate the girls I dated to get what I wanted.

When I met Chasity I knew I had met the woman I was supposed to spend the rest of my life with. But I was still stuck by habit with using her. And I thought this was normal.

Wife and Husband

Chasity: As we read John Paul II's theology of the body, I came across certain passages that would, if only briefly, free me from my past chains. I felt liberated, clean, and whole, if only for a moment. I specifically remember one evening when I came across a specific passage and yelled out to Mike, "The pope rocks!"

As time went on, we began to open our hearts to God more and more. We prayed for him to work in our lives, to transform us, to make us whole. He began healing us, or should I say we were finally receptive to healing, beginning with confronting the death of Cullen.

God helped us realize that Cullen had served a divine purpose in his short life. He had brought us to Jesus, broken and on our knees, crying out for God to embrace us and make us whole again. Our little one brought us a miracle—all before he was born. And he was rewarded with eternal life with our Lord.

Mike: Not until I learned about the theology of the body did I realize the true potential of sex and how diabolically wrong I had been about it. It was as if I had been blind. Now God gave me new eyes, and I could see for the first time.

My big shortcomings were easy to see. I gave up pornography and masturbation, by God's grace. Then I began to evaluate how sincere my gift of self was and tried to deprogram from the way I had operated in the past.

As my wife was facing her abusive past, I had to reflect on my own inclinations. It made me nauseous to think that I had operated with similar intentions to those of the guys who had wounded her so deeply. With a new openness to God's mercy and a process of reflection, purging, and healing, I am now on the road to discovering what it means to be a true man.

Beloved and Lover

Chasity: It didn't happen overnight, but gradually, as we learned more about the theology of the body and continued to open our hearts to God, I began to find healing and peace within. For the first time I knew that my body, for the sole reason that I was created in the image and likeness of God, had great dignity and should never be used for another's selfish desires. I began incorporating the teachings into my life, simultaneously healing from my past and living my married life as God had intended. I was able to give myself to Mike completely.

The more Mike and I entered into the marital embrace the way God intended it, the closer I came to true purity. For the first times in our lives, we were encountering God in all aspects of our marriage, and we were joyfully singing his praises.

There are days when the demons from the past try to rear their ugly heads. I still struggle with them. But through the grace of God, this is now a battle Mike and I recognize and are equipped to fight.

Mike: I slowly began to identify myself with the real man, Jesus Christ, and let go of all the false idols—mainly sports stars and actors—to whom I had clung from boyhood in a desperate attempt to discover true masculinity. I learned through the theology of the body that my role as a man is not only to provide my wife with physical protection from outside threats but to safeguard her inner dignity. This means I must evaluate my intentions each and every time we come together in the marital embrace, and I must respect her freedom to accept my gift offering or reject it. This is very liberating.

I have discovered the true meaning behind my innate desire to be the protector of my wife, and I have learned how to love her as Christ loved us on the cross. Although it has been a difficult journey and continues to be a daily challenge, I find strength in reflecting on Ephesians 5:25: "Husbands, love your wives, as Christ loved the Church and gave himself up for her."

One in Christ

We celebrated our seventh wedding anniversary in December 2009. It has also been seven years since we snuck into the singles' meeting and first heard about the transforming truth of the theology of the body. Both days mark milestones in our lives:

Our anniversary commemorates the day we gave ourselves to one another in holy matrimony, while the date we first heard of the theology of the body celebrates the beginning of our journey to discover how to be true gifts to each other. Thanks to the teachings of John Paul II, our lives are drastically different from what they might have been. We are glad we opened our hearts and listened to God's inviting whisper.

For so long we subscribed to the deceptions that we had been fed. Like sheep following one another without purpose, we believed the lies and found ways to rationalize our actions when our consciences tugged at us. Now we try to take on each new day with a sense of service and donation to the other.

We are grateful to God for the gifts of our three children, Anthony, Jacob, and Mary Grace. They serve as constant reminders of the complete gift of self Christ gave to us on the cross, and they help us live our lives in service to him.

. . . .

Mike and Chasity Short lead small groups that study the theology of the body and are active in TOBET. They live in Fort Worth, Texas.

. . . .

CHAPTER | **T H R E E**

ABUNDANT LIFE

R.J.

On the day that Pope John Paul II died, I cried nearly as much as I did when my father passed away the year before. I had never met the pope or even seen him in person, so to some this might seem absurd. However, through the guidance of the Holy Spirit, the words of his papacy had personally touched my heart and changed my life. His words, particularly his theology of the body, gave me a renewed sense of trust and hope in God's plan for me, as well as an awe and appreciation for what Jesus has established in the rock of the Catholic Church.

Talk About Sex

I grew up in what could be called a typical Catholic home. My family attended Mass together every Sunday. I became active in the youth group, and through a powerful retreat experience in the tenth grade, I drew closer to Jesus and wanted to spend my life following him. However, though I loved the Lord, my young spiritual roots were seldom nurtured with solid Catholic teaching, particularly about sexuality. These roots would prove too shallow to withstand the temptations of the world.

15

Through my teenage years I heard several talks about sex. Most of the adults in my life deeply cared for my soul, so they delivered the best messages about sex they could. I appreciate their efforts, because I see how their words helped to form my conscience. The message was simple: Sex outside of marriage is a sin, dangerous and regrettable. My mother often spoke about how grateful she was that she never "gave in" to those guys who were no longer part of her life.

Guest speakers at youth group discussed the joy of waiting until marriage, also reiterating that no one else could share that part of them besides their spouse. Most speakers, church and secular, endlessly warned of the dangers of sexually transmitted diseases and the "burden" of pregnancy and babies. Still others made unflattering remarks about girls who became pregnant out of wedlock. Some talked about women who had abortions because of unplanned pregnancies. All of the messages strongly said, "Don't do it."

At the time I was strongly convinced, but as time passed these messages left little evidence to persuade this hard-headed teen-ager. While the world said sex was something good, all I heard from Christians about sex was negative. It was at this time of my life that I needed to hear the good news of the theology of the body. But I didn't.

Toward the end of my junior year, I began dating a smart and funny athlete, the class president, who was known as a good guy from a good family, and was even Catholic. As is the case with many young couples, our relationship began in joy and innocence, as two high schoolers grew in affection for one another. But after several months of dating, it became difficult to withstand the physical temptations. Though I had been taught that sex outside of marriage was wrong, I easily ignored my conscience on sins against chastity that didn't include intercourse.

I knew what the world expected of my relationship with this guy. If I decided to have sex, I would take that big step that most of my friends already had. We were not from our parents' generation, where sex outside of marriage was a shameful act that was guarded as top secret. Rather it had become a rite of passage for young women in high school.

Internally I refuted almost every point that I had been taught about sex. My mind believed the world, and I considered one sexual partner for life a thing of the past. I also easily dismissed my possibilities for sexually transmitted diseases, pregnancy, and abortion. With all of my public education about contraception, I knew I had little to lose as long as I "was safe" with "protection."

·At this point I had never heard about the Church's teaching regarding contraception. I had even heard many Catholics discuss the importance of "safe sex." They would remark, "I don't suggest you have sex outside of marriage, but if you do it, be safe."

My internal conflict was paradoxical, because I could not grasp how such a natural and loving act could be so wrong and against the will of God. My boyfriend and I believed we truly loved each other, and there was little to stop us from moving ahead.

Crossing the Line

We had sex, and what followed was a downhill road of sin and pain. After a two-year relationship, we broke up. I was heart-broken, and only later would I realize the role that the unifying act of sex played in my heartbreak.

Little did I know that my next relationship would begin physically where the prior one had left off. In college, sex became commonplace. As with any other sin, my avoidance of the reconciliation and continuation of the sin led to a dulled conscience. Sex became a typical thing that came with the few serious relationships I had.

On the outside it seemed I had everything a young woman could want. I made the dean's list or president's list every semester. As college graduation approached, my college internships were pointing toward a successful career in television and public relations. I had beauty, youth, and a serious relationship with a successful man.

But I was sad and unfulfilled. I numbed the emptiness in my life with a nonstop nightlife of parties, alcohol, and red-carpet treatment at the best clubs and social events. And surprisingly, through it all I rarely missed Mass on Sunday morning. I still considered myself a "good Catholic."

Looking back, I clearly see how it was my strong deviation from God's will that led to my unhappiness and pain. I did not know how beautifully and wonderfully made I was. I did not know that I was made for true communion with God and others through being a gift for others. Rather I was using others and allowing myself to be used—the opposite of true love.

The unhealthy relationships became a wide door through which jealously, anger, and shame entered my life, as well as sexually transmitted disease. I felt unsatisfied by the treatment that I received in relationships, although the world said my decisions about sexual freedom made me a strong and independent woman. And as I became more dependent on the world's standards, the unthinkable happened.

After a couple of missed periods, some nausea, and a pregnancy test, I knew I had conceived a child. My use of contraception, particularly birth control pills, had so broken the connection between sex and pregnancy that I had thought myself invincible. The pregnancy came as a shock—and a source of panic and fear.

One thing I believed from the many talks I had heard as a teenager: A baby was a burden, and this pregnancy would obstruct all of my dreams. Ironically I thought, "Me, the front-row Catholic? What will people say?" I was ashamed of what my family, including my church family, would think of me. I didn't want my life to become a teaching tool for others.

I chose to have an abortion in order to "remove" this "obstacle." What I would experience through this decision would be much more horrific than becoming a source of criticism, but I was naive. To this day, over ten years after my abortion, I grieve for my child, who lives on in my memories and daily thoughts.

The Oasis in the Desert

God's grace became apparent through a turn of events in my life during the year 2000, the year of the Jubilee. I moved to go to graduate school, painfully leaving my family, friends, and boyfriend. With the pressures of a full-time job and homework, I could not visit home as much as I wanted. I spent many nights sad and lonely, no longer the weekend socialite that I had been in my hometown. Little did I know that God was taking me into the desert, alone and broken, that I might rediscover his love for me.

In my loneliness I desired friends, and I stumbled onto an amazing community at the university's Catholic student center. (I was not necessarily searching for Catholic friends, but God knew what I needed.) I found these new friends to be serious and committed Christians amid the hedonistic college environment. They loved God and were serious about following him. They could have fun without drunkenness, hook-ups, and shame.

I was lured by the joy and lifestyle of these new friends and began to let go of my old friends and ways. To the chagrin of my boyfriend, I ended our four-year relationship. I had become convinced that a future with him was not part of God's will for my life.

During the course of this conversion experience, God led me to the words of Pope John Paul II's theology of the body. My mind began to move from false "truths" to real truth, from confusion to understanding, from pain to healing. The realization of God's intense love for me came through this new understanding of his original purpose for my body. Before, I had thought, "Sex is bad." But the pope taught me that sex is good and even holy. He taught me that sex reflects God but only when used correctly, as the gift of one person to another and of both to God.

What changed me most was the concept of *giving* versus *grasping*. The pope refers to Philippians 2 to show how Jesus did not *grasp* but *gave* of himself completely. This concept has shaped how I view not just the purpose of sex but the purpose of life in general.

Today's world describes love as feeling-oriented romance, mixed with flowers, diamonds, and nice gestures. I had chased the world's version of love, but romantic feelings came and went, my flowers died, and the guys who said nice things and gave me diamonds treated me as an object—and I used them as well. The worldly version of love brought me nothing but pain and a lack of meaning.

Pope John Paul II led me to seek only Christ's exemplary gift of love, which is *total* giving and sacrifice. I began to better understand real love and to see marital love and sex as a total gift of oneself, which beautifully emulates Christ's total gift of himself for me. I realized that I had settled for counterfeit versions of love throughout my life, but God was offering me so much more than empty imitations. Once I understood this, my whole world changed.

Today, by God's grace, I am living an abundant life (see John 10:10). I am in a joyful, fruitful marriage with a man who loves God dearly and believes in imitating Christ's total gift of self, therefore loving me better than any ways I could have dreamed of in the past. I have begun the process of healing my past wounds.

Our marriage has also been tremendously blessed with beautiful children. I had thought babies were burdens and expensive commodities for married people, so I "responsibly" wanted only one or two. John Paul II taught me that separating sex from procreation denies God's gift of sex. I now know that this sacred act reflects the Holy Trinity and allows *our love* to take part in God's powerful act of creation. Sex in our Catholic marriage allows us to give ourselves completely to each other, with no barriers (such as contraceptives) in the way, as Christ gave himself *completely* to us.

Our children do require great sacrifices, but our sacrifices are opportunities to be molded into the image of Jesus. Our openness to God's gift of children is also an opportunity for us to rely and trust in the providence of God. To this day God has never failed to provide for any of our needs. If only I had known years ago what I know now.

It is no wonder that many people of my generation cried at the loss of the beloved Pope John Paul II. We lost a father who gave us a sense of hope and meaning by opening up God's words to us in a new, direct, and profound way. Thanks to God, we know that John Paul the Great continues to intercede for us in heaven, that we may bring this message of hope and renewal to the next generation.

. . . .

TRANSFORMED
Anonymous

"Am I ever going to change?" I asked myself this question many times throughout my life.

I am a twenty-four-year-old male who has struggled with issues of same-sex attraction. Most of my early life was dominated by fear and confusion concerning my sexuality. Then a conversion to Christ and an encounter with the theology of the body changed my life forever. I certainly *have* changed: God has recreated me in a whole new way.

Experimentation, Fear, Frustration

When I was about eight years old, a new family moved in across the street. I made friends with one of the boys from this family, and soon we started to experiment with each other sexually. Those encounters were my first experiences of both the pleasure sexuality could bring and the way it could affect relationships.

While these experiences were exciting, I felt intense anxiety about my relationship with this boy. I knew nothing about human sexuality, what it meant to be "gay," or what was considered appropriate and moral sexual behavior. But I knew in my heart that something was not right with this experimentation. The other boy shared my sense that we could not have these encounters out in the open, so we kept them secret.

I still remember the intense feeling of fear that rushed over me as I walked home from one of our sleepovers. I wished I could go back in time and prevent any of these encounters from ever happening. In the back of my mind, I intuited that sexuality was a gift meant for more than just pleasure.

For the next ten years I lived in fear of my sexuality. Throughout middle school I watched other boys develop attractions to girls. I wondered why I did not seem to have the same desires. Despite the encounters of my early youth, I was dominated more by fear of girls than by attraction to boys. I always felt as if I were an outsider looking in on everyone else exploring the opposite sex. I wondered why I was afraid of the thought of kissing a girl and why it was all such a struggle.

Every Sunday I asked God to fix what was wrong with me. I prayed to be "normal."

Depression and Addiction

Moving into my high school years, my sexual anxiety and confusion slowly turned into depression. I felt more alone than ever. I kept telling myself that I was a freak, and no one would or could ever understand what I was going through.

The world of men seemed foreign to me as I struggled to keep up a strong façade in the all-male school I attended. I participated in sports mostly to avoid ridicule. I always felt inadequate and had very little sense of my own masculinity. I never considered myself a man; I thought I was hardly a boy.

As I moved through puberty, my ambivalence toward women slowly turned into attraction toward men. I was deeply ashamed of this attraction and did my best to hide it. Being "outed" at an all-male high school would have been the worst possible thing that could happen to me. I lived in fear of locker-rooms and other such situations; I was never comfortable around other males when naked.

By this time I had discovered masturbation and pornography. I would escape to the basement of my house, hoping that I could catch a TV program that featured nudity. The excitement of seeing men having sex with women (or each other), combined with the intense pleasure of masturbation, created an unbelievably powerful "drug" that took hold of my life.

I knew that the Catholic Church spoke against masturbation and pornography, so I tried to control my habit. However, when temptations arose it felt nearly impossible to say no. I would often debate with myself, one part of me cognizant of the fact that masturbation was wrong, and the other part of me kicking, screaming, and rationalizing at every turn for the sexual release. My habit was taking over my life.

The worst episode of my high school years came near the end of my sophomore year. A kid who had been bullying me since elementary school started a rumor that I had been caught masturbating in the bathroom. Worse, the rumor had me masturbating with our high school yearbook. You can imagine the implications of being caught with the yearbook at an all-male school.

I still remember walking into the cafeteria that day. It seemed as if I could hear everyone talking about me behind my back. Even my closest friends at the lunch table believed the rumor. All of my worst fears were realized: I had been exposed as the freak that I was convinced I was. I hung my head low that day, acting as if I really had been caught in the act.

The same bully started another rumor that I was gay because I wore a pea coat to school. I wondered if my life could get any worse.

Although I had many friends and was very successful in school and extracurricular activities, the problem with my sexuality seemed to overshadow everything. I did not love myself. I often contemplated suicide but never made any attempts. I had a girlfriend for a few months, and I truly enjoyed spending time with her, but the relationship was a lot more about putting up a "normal" face than about being in a romantic relationship.

Same-sex attractions remained prevalent in my life; in fact, I lusted after any man who was physically fit and appeared or acted strong. I think that deep down I wanted to feel as strong as others looked, so I clung to my penchant for the "perfect" man. I still prayed to be "normal" and find myself physically attracted to women.

Joy and Transformation

During my senior year, my brother and a few classmates suggested that I attend a four-day retreat. It was here that my prayers to be "normal" would finally be answered, but not in the way that I had imagined.

As I stepped off the bus at the retreat center, I was immediately greeted by the retreat team, a few teachers, but mostly my peers. "It's great to see you here," and, "So glad you could make it, man," were some of the things they said. It was refreshing to be welcomed instead of rejected. My classmates' acceptance, so different from their treatment of me in the hallways at school, helped me lower my guard.

In our first small group meeting, we talked about our expectations for the retreat and for our lives in general. One of the group leaders told us that now was the time to let it all out. He told us not to hold back if we wanted to get something out of the retreat.

As soon as the words came out of his mouth, I knew that this might be my chance to reveal everything that I was going through. I was in a protected environment, an authentic brother-hood. Of course, another part of me was fearful that I would be subject to even more ridicule and rejection.

My conversion to Christ occurred sometime during the late evening of October 29, 2003. I read a letter from my mother, which triggered something inside me. She told me how much she loved me and how proud she was of all my accomplishments.

How could I have been so blind? There was love all around me, from my family and from all of my brothers on this retreat. The joy quite literally came pouring down from heaven, and I felt completely engulfed in the presence of God. I saw different episodes of my life and realized that every single moment, every breath, everything, led up to this event. I realized that God was with me every step of the way, and Jesus was waiting for me with open arms.

A day later I found myself in our small group again. People were sharing some very intense stories from their lives. Finally it came down to me. My heart was pounding against my chest, and my entire body was in a state of emotional overload. I debated endlessly with myself.

With tears welling up in my eyes, I looked to one side and saw my group leader signal to the other leader that we were not done yet. My struggle was obvious, and he knew that there was something I desperately needed to get off my chest. To this day I am convinced that he would have kept us there all night until I let it all out.

The moment came, and I just put it all out there. I do not remember exactly what I said, but I explained the intense pain and fear that I had felt all my life. My sexuality was in shambles, and I had no idea who I was.

Immediately I felt like a completely different person. It was in that moment—when I was exposed, felt the weakest, and had my guard down—that I was simultaneously the strongest I had ever been. I had the courage to break through the chains of oppression that I had built for myself, and the process of healing could now begin.

My peers did not mock me but affirmed my struggle, and some even shared how they had felt many of the emotions that I was experiencing. I no longer had to be alone on this journey. The group showed me that it was possible to reveal myself to others without fear of rejection. I promised myself to never let fear hold me down again.

After that retreat my desire to masturbate was nearly eradicated, and I can only attribute this to the deliverance of Jesus Christ. I ousted pornography from my life, and it was as if the most gigantic weight was lifted right off my shoulders. Although I still had many questions about my sexuality and same-sex attractions, for once I felt as if I was ready to live my life.

Finding the Theology of the Body

I faced many challenges in college, but with my faith firmly established, I had an entirely new way of coping with hardship. I could offer all of my struggles to God instead of internalizing them into a little bottle of depression and anxiety. I even started to have feelings for a young woman, though a relationship never materialized.

I continued to question my sexuality. It almost seemed as if God was telling me that I was gay. Then I heard the message of the theology of the body.

My best friend at that time was my roommate, a man who helped me grow much closer to Christ. He lent me his collection of CDs on the theology of the body. I will never forget the first time I listened to them. I was folding my laundry when I heard: "If we are afraid of our sexuality, then the devil has already won."

I dropped what I was doing and just stood there for a second. It dawned on me: I had been living in fear of my sexuality for my entire life!

I became extremely interested in what the theology of the body might have to say for someone in my situation. I learned that Christopher West, a national speaker on the theology of the body, would be speaking near my college, so my roommate and I bought tickets and planned a road trip.

Christopher spoke about what the Bible says about the marriage of man and woman. He also talked about the lies and confusion we buy into and about the devil's hell-bent efforts to obscure the gift of our sexuality. I had a million questions going through my mind.

I wondered if my same-sex attractions had nothing to do with being "gay" but rather resulted from confusion about what it really means to be a man. Our culture sends all sorts of mixed messages, on the one hand saying that homosexuality is to be celebrated while on the other hand ridiculing homosexuals in commercials, TV shows, and movies. I thought about my intuitions as a child that my early homosexual encounters were not right.

After Christopher spoke, he was kind enough to meet with anyone willing to wait to see him. While in line with my friend, that same old debate turned on in my head: Was I really going to mention my same-sex attraction in public, not to mention right next to my best friend? The scene reminded me of my inner debate at the retreat: Would I reveal these secrets to my small group?

I then recalled my promise to never be governed by fear, and I knew that I would have to put it all out there. My heart beating wildly again, I barely stammered out the words: "How do I deal with same-sex attraction?"

Christopher immediately thanked me for my courage. He proceeded to affirm, "First and foremost, you are a man."

"Whoa," I thought to myself. Not only had I never heard those words before, but this was the first time in my life that I truly felt like a man. Once again it was when I was at my weakest and most exposed that I felt closest to God and my true self.

I began to read and learn about the theology of the body and the theories behind the development of same-sex attractions. I read many testimonials of men who had struggled with this issue, and it seemed as if they were telling my own biography. I was not alone.

I started learning to love the man that I was and stopped trying to be the man that I was not. I was not the greatest athlete, but God had blessed me with an intellectual mind-set, so I learned to cherish my studies. I embraced one of my other passions, music, and aggressively set out to better my skills as a singer and guitarist.

The biggest success, however, came from combining what I learned in the theology of the body with the sacraments of the

Catholic Church. I started attending daily Mass and receiving the Eucharist day in and day out. I realized that this was what I had been looking for all along! If I really wanted to learn what it meant to be a man, how much further did I need to look than the Sacrament of the greatest man who ever lived? Many of the same-sex attractions started to fade.

I recognized the distorted image I had of what it meant to be a man. The real man is not massively muscular and well-groomed; he is bloody and weak on a cross. Jesus Christ became and continues to be the only man I will ever need.

Living the Theology of the Body

In my final two years of college, I continued to grow in my faith and understanding my masculinity. The theology of the body helped me uncover the true beauty of both married and celibate life.

After graduation I opted to do a year of service rather than immediately start a career. I wanted to discern my vocation as well as consider working full-time in theology-of-the-body evangelization. I moved to the other side of the country and started volunteering with a theology-of-the-body think tank.

The Lord placed numerous people and experiences in front of me during my time there; it was exactly what I needed when I needed it. I developed a strong friendship with a woman who was a beautiful instrument of healing in my life. I learned how to receive the love of a woman and integrate my *eros* rather than repress it. Having such a pure friendship taught me how to love being a man, and for the first time in my life, I stopped running away from marriage. My wounds had convinced me that I was not "man enough" to be a father, but this beautiful relationship untwisted that distortion.

The truth is that God created me for fatherhood, be it physical or spiritual. Although I am broken and wounded, the Lord will give me the grace I need.

Numerous encounters with awesome priests and married couples continued to heal my wounds, and I continued to grow in my desire to be an instrument of Christ for others. I hope that my past struggles will prepare me to be a wounded healer for the world. Regardless of my vocation, I am no longer afraid to be a man of God; I love the gift of my masculinity! Whether single, married, or celibate, I pray that I may always help others uncover the truth of their glorious creation as male or female and the call to offer their bodies as gifts for others.

"Am I ever going to change?" Through the love of Christ and the power of God's grace, I now have an answer to this question: "I have already been transformed." My life is a testament to the fact that authentic healing from the distortions of human sexuality is not only possible but necessary. If we remain open to God's grace and the Lord's initiative in our lives, anything is possible.

As I continue to discover the true meaning of my creation as a man, I humbly ask for your prayers. And if you struggle with your sexuality, please know that I am praying for you. Be not afraid, for the Lord wants to transform you into the man or woman he created you to be.

. . . .

THIS IS MY BODY:
THE MOST IMPORTANT WORDS IN THE UNIVERSE
Monica A. Ashour

Once while in Rome, I got trapped in the catacombs. Yes, you read that correctly—*trapped* in the catacombs, the underground, cave-like tunnels where the early Christians used to go to escape persecution.

Two friends and I arrived at the catacombs, but we had missed the last tour. Marcia, luckily, decided to rest while Ray and I looked around. We came upon a door that was unlocked, so we went in, and then we saw another door. We needed no words; we're both adventurous. We went through the door, and there before our eyes was a statue of St. Cecilia. We were in the catacombs!

Without a guide, we began looking around at the fantastic place. Then Ray prudently said, "Monica, we better retrace our steps, since the early Christians used to get lost in these endless miles of tunnels." So we did. And there was our newfound, official guide, St. Cecilia.

We went on, even as Ray expressed his concern. Then the lights went off! "Oh, my gosh, oh, my gosh!" I screamed. It was pitch-black! I imagined scooting aside some bones of a dead person so I could sleep in the same cubby, or starving to death, or running out of oxygen.

Ray encouraged me: "Calm down. We know the way back."

We attempted the route we had memorized—or thought we had memorized—to no avail. We were lost. We were stuck. We were afraid.

"Whistle, Monica, whistle!"

Little had I known that the talent of whistling loudly, which I developed in junior high, would save my life one day! After a while we heard Marcia: "Monica! Ray!"

"We're here!" we responded.

Marcia had found a tour guide, and he, with a terrified look on his face, had been trying to convince her that it was impossible for us to be down there. After more whistling so he could find us, I was greeted with hugs and tears from Marcia and a slap on the cheek from the guide. "I could have gone to jail!" he fumed.

"Sorry, so sorry!"

He forgave us, gave us a grand tour by flashlight, and gave us religious medals when we went above ground.

Why do I begin with this tale? I think it serves as a terrific symbol of what the theology of the body did for me and can do for our Church and all of society.

First, I consider much of my life before hearing the theology of the body to be a time of darkness. I was trapped in a seemingly inescapable shell of selfishness, with little self-understanding.

Second, St. Cecilia and all the saints who have gone on before us lived out the most important words in the universe, "This is my body," even to the point of death.

Next, an outward expression of my body (whistling) revealed where I was.

Lastly, the tour guide's slap is representative of what the theology of the body did for me: It jolted me out of myself, leading me to true freedom (symbolized by the friendly tour of the catacombs), allowing me better to love and teach others about this life-changing message.

This Is My Body: The Incarnate Body of Our Lord

Jesus had to learn what it meant to be a body-person, and so do we. As I tried to mine the truths of the theology of the body, such as "the language of the body"[1] and being aware of the "movements" of my heart,[2] I pondered what these words might mean, while asking Our Lady for her help. We are not to be afraid of, disregard, or elevate our bodies; rather we ought to embrace them for what they are: "sacraments" of persons.[3] Our bodies reveal our inner life; our bodies reveal *us*, just as Jesus in his own incarnate body revealed himself.

From that small yet immensely dense concept, I became different.

I am ashamed to say that I was a good liar; I didn't think lying was that big a deal. But the theology of the body taught me that anytime I know a certain truth in my heart, I ought never to violate that truth or myself or the person who deserves the truth. Cardinal Joseph Ratzinger (now our beloved Pope Benedict XVI) obviously understood this point when he coined the term *un-be*. I realized via the theology of the body that I was *un-being* myself anytime I lied.

This is one aspect of what it means to be a body-person: I should never allow the spiritual dimension of my life—my interior self—to be split or unhinged from my bodily actions. Pope John Paul II put it this way: There should be "no inner break and antithesis between what is spiritual and what is sensible."[4] I am an integral composite of body and soul.

This reminded me of what I had learned as a graduate student about the heresy of Gnosticism, which says that because Jesus was divine, he was not actually also human; he merely *appeared* to be human. This heresy denies that Christ had a human body, and diminishes the body's meaning. The Church rightly condemned this heresy long ago. I had not realized, however, until learning the theology of the body, that I was guilty of being Gnostic because I did not think that my body had a deeper meaning attached to it.

For example, I used to think that just praying about something was sufficient, but that discounted the God-given gift of reason; now I pray and think about things. I also previously thought that I was deeply spiritual because I did not bother about my clothing and thought makeup was superficial. The theology of the body showed me that feminine attire—flattering without being seductive—is not only justified, but also proper. My feminine body reveals my feminine soul.

That sin is the rupture between a pure soul and bodily actions struck me like a lightning bolt. All I needed to do was cooperate with God's grace in helping me not to "split" myself. Pope John Paul II called this idea "virginal value."[5]

This opened up for me a new way to look at the dogma of Mary's perpetual virginity. I realized that Mary was virginal in the normal sense of the word, but she was also virginal insofar as every one of her bodily actions conformed to her pure heart. She always lived as an integrated person. Her body and soul always corresponded.

This is holiness! Sanctity, then, seemed actually attainable. If I lived an integrated life, given a pure heart, then I could grow to sainthood.

I began to notice the "movements of the heart." My heart would say, "No, don't do that; that is gossip," "Watch her downcast eyes; ask her if she is OK," "You are about to exaggerate; just tell the truth." Over and over again my heart convicted me, and I tried to follow such convictions with bodily actions.

I discovered through the theology of the body that when I listen to my pure heart, I am becoming the true me. As I said in one of my presentations recently, "I feel like a woman of steel," that is, working on not letting anything unclean from outside—to paraphrase our Lord—bend me. Yet simultaneously my heart continues to be pliable, open more and more to others. The dark catacombs that trapped me are being lit up as I am guided to freedom.

This Is My Body: The Eucharistic Body of Our Lord

What wonderful hope I felt in learning these simple truths from the theology of the body. As the darkness was lifting, however, I found that I was still "splitting" myself.

Then I read the Holy Father's words about the sacraments "infusing grace"[6] into us and his words on life in the Spirit. These were a slap on the face, for sure. We Catholics know that we must cooperate with God, but it is his action that changes us. Pope John Paul II says, "In this struggle between good and evil, man proves to be *stronger thanks to the power of the Holy Spirit who*, working within the human spirit, causes *its desires to bear fruit in the good*."[7] The battle within could be won.

Silently calling on the Holy Spirit, often in front of people who do not know I am praying, has become a big part of my life. I also remember one time in particular when I continued falling into a stupid temptation, until I finally asked Jesus to help. He did. I found freedom, true freedom, thanks to the work of the Holy Spirit. Self-mastery feels so good, much better than giving in to the angry outbursts and evil intentions that used to trap me.

Certainly my friends, family, spiritual director of seventeen years—Auxiliary Bishop Mark Seitz of Dallas—(and I) will tell you that I am far from perfect. But they will tell you of the peace and joy that overwhelm me now. I am convinced that it is Pope John Paul's message that began a revolution in me, solidified by my participation at daily Mass, to which I bring all the events and people in my life and from which I draw life and love-giving sustenance.

When I studied Pope John Paul's explanation of the parallel between marital love and our union with Christ at Mass, I was changed radically. As a single person, I still benefit from this parallel, for I know I am ratifying my baptismal vows when I am united with my Bridegroom eucharistically, just as a married couple ratify their wedding vows when they become one flesh. I know that Jesus longs for me much more than I long for him. What a secure feeling and a sure foundation he gives me! I am loved.

Now that I have immersed myself in the theology of the body, I rarely go a day without at least thirty minutes of Eucharistic Adoration. I approach God with a feminine heart, the deepest part of me. No longer am I in darkness, but rather I am in touch with the deepest part of my being, living in the depths of God himself: Father, Son, and Holy Spirit.

This Is My Body: The Mystical Body of Our Lord

My goal is to know the Father, Son, and Holy Spirit and live in their exchange of life and love. I knew this fantastic concept, the true foundation of Christianity, but it came alive for me when I studied the theology of the body. That study awakened in me a vision of Christianity I had never seen before.

Not only do I live *in* Jesus when I share in his incarnation by being a body-person; not only do I live *in* Jesus when I share in his Eucharistic Body; but I also live *in* Jesus when I form a communion of persons with others. Ultimately we all—every one of us in the communion of saints—live *in* each other as well, starting now![8] Unbelievable!

I thus realized that when I give the gift of myself to others, I become more me precisely because others then dwell in me. Just as the Father, Son, and Holy Spirit always delight in each other, so my family and friends delight in each other. I have a taste of the eternal delight in God when I have "golden sessions," to use C.S. Lewis's term about his friendships,[9] with my closest friends, Dayspring, Alyssan, and DeAnn, or when I take a walk with my nieces and nephews. And I feel like a tabernacle containing the sacredness of another after someone shares his or her story with me after one of my talks. Time seems to stand still in the wonder of such union and communion. This is the theology of the body lived.

Pope John Paul underscores the truth of our being made for a communion of persons when he speaks of the vowed life: marriage and consecrated life. In both, he maintains, understanding who we are—either in our masculinity or in our femininity—is vital. That marriage is the best natural sign of who God is in his inner life complements the supernatural sign of heaven shown in religious life and the priesthood.

Learning this fostered my teaching tremendously. For instance, instead of only giving the philosophical argument that the two ends of marital love are union and procreation, I now use Pope

John Paul's understanding that the ultimate reason for the marital embrace is the *total* gift of self. Contraception's message is the opposite of total gift: I am holding something back (I am not completely vulnerable to you); I don't accept you totally (I refuse your fertility); I don't trust you (I need "protection").

Please do not misunderstand me. I do not condemn people who have used contraception, but I do give them the truth. Often couples say to me privately, with deep sadness and sometimes fierce anger, "Why have we never been told this? This is fantastic! What shall we do?" The darkness of their ignorance is striking, but the truth sets us all free.

I also learned from the theology of the body that marital love "in some sense becomes liturgical,"[10] a form of worshiping God! No longer, "Just say no till you are married." Marital love is so sacred that we would never want to desecrate it. When I teach this concept to married couples, invariably a husband, with a wry smile, will take his wife's hand and say, "Honey, let's go worship God!" We women always want men to be spiritual leaders; they are finally stepping up!

This leads me to another eye-opening, life-changing concept of the theology of the body: The opposite of love is not hatred but the use of others. I could see that I used my parents, calling them only when I needed something. I used the grocery store clerk and the bank teller, looking at them as objects, not as people. I used my friends, caring only for my agenda and my needs. I even used God, going to him all too often for this or that, not "just because."

Don't get me wrong: We should go to God and other people and ask for their help. But we should not use them as means to our ends.

This opposition between love and use was particularly eye-opening for my students. That and other concepts of the theology of the body enabled me to transform my teachings into a living mosaic, synthesizing various Church doctrines and subjects into one piece.

Of one piece, too, is how we are to all live. Living in a communion of persons as the Mystical Body of Christ is how we reflect God's inner life of love the most. I try my best to give the gift of self at all times in my life and in my speaking, just as the tour guide in the catacombs gave us the gift of a grand tour.

The Most Important Words in the Universe

The early Christian martyrs were buried in the catacombs after loving God so much that they shed their blood and gave up their bodies for him. My "catacombs"—deception, selfishness—were the opposite of such self-sacrifice. The theology of the body excavated in me the truth of love, that the gift of self builds the Mystical Body of Christ, even as I find myself in such a gift.

When I live as a body-person, filled with my Eucharistic Lord, I am in the "center" of the Church, as Pope Benedict invites us to be. His predecessor and friend, our beloved Pope John Paul II, gave us a message of life and freedom that so changed me that my life's work is to convey this message of hope.

The late Holy Father called his work "the basis of the most appropriate method...of man's education."[11] The "tour" of the theology of the body was and is the best I have ever taken. I pray that it may jolt many people out of the darkness of complacency and sin, to bring true joy and happiness, here and throughout eternity.

May we, with our Lord and Our Lady, say, "This is my body, given."

. . . .

Monica Ashour holds masters degrees in theological studies and humanities from the University of Dallas. She is a full-time theology of the body speaker and the executive director for the Theology of the Body Evangelization Team, Inc. (TOBET), a non-profit organization (www.tobet.org). She also serves as an online instructor for Homeschool Connections (http://homeschoolconnectionsonline.com).
She can be reached at mashour@tobet.org.

. . . .

PURE FREEDOM
Casey

My family did many of the things that Catholic families do, and we called ourselves Catholic, but I don't think any of us were really aware of what the Church taught, and I know for sure that this is specifically true in the field of human sexuality. I needed the truth of the theology of the body.

I was never given a "birds and bees" talk, and now that I recognize my parents' lack of knowledge of the Church's teaching on the subject at the time, I'm glad they didn't give me one. Still I learned from what they implicitly taught our family. I've always had a strong desire to be a husband someday—and not just a husband but a *good* husband, one who really loves his wife and treats her properly.

For the most part my father treated my mother very well (and vice versa), but I saw other men who didn't treat women well, and it bothered me. As I grew up, however, I knew that something was wrong with the way my parents viewed sexuality. Since they never gave me "the talk," I started to learn about sex on my own—or rather, I started to learn what the culture taught about sexuality.

Broken

My parents divorced while I was in junior high, and their communication after that was all but nonexistent. This certainly didn't help my parents guide my siblings and me. A few years later my brother said that my dad's advice to him was, "Just don't get a girl pregnant." This, of course, was just what my brother wanted to hear—his father's more or less full consent for sexual recklessness.

Something about my father's advice didn't sit well with me. Yet there were many factors in my life that formed in me a worldly view of marriage and sex. In junior high I was exposed to pornography, and by the time high school came, I was addicted to viewing explicit imagery. My primary way of seeing a woman was not a loving way but a lustful one. Deep down I knew there was a more laudable way to appreciate women, and I tried to keep my focus in proper areas, but I consistently failed.

Somebody gave my brother and me a CD of explicit images, which we saved on our computer. We both became adept at hiding the files—making them invisible or putting them in a complicated series of subfolders. We both lived primarily with our mother, and she never thought to check the computer for such imagery—nor would she have known how. I used the images so frequently that, to this day, I have to keep strict watch over my thoughts.

Late in high school the pornography began to shape my mind. Having intercourse with a woman was what I desired, yet I knew it was wrong to have sex outside of marriage, and I truly wanted a healthy and lasting relationship. Looking back, I don't think that would have been at all possible at the time. Thankfully, God prevented any woman in whom I was romantically interested from returning my interest.

The constant pressures from my inner desires, raging hormones, pornography, my friends' behaviors, the imagery from TV and movies, and the ideas behind popular music all fought against a little notion inside of me that premarital sex wouldn't be right. I am truly thankful for what little instruction on sexual morality was given through our school, because it helped stir my conscience. I wish I had been able to experience the truths of John Paul II's theology of the body earlier, so I could have known the *proper* way to appreciate a woman instead of just knowing that there *was* a proper way.

Eventually I started to masturbate—an instant problem that would continue for seven years. I had never heard the Church's stance on the spiritual dangers of masturbation; the only thing I did hear was a friend's incorrect statement that the Church taught that it was tolerable. I didn't fully believe this, but I used it to excuse my behavior.

Nevertheless, God kept working on my conscience. I could tell, deep down, that there was something wrong with what I was doing. I would challenge myself to see how long I could resist. Some times were better than others, but I was still caught.

A Ray of Hope

In college the problems only grew worse. Shortly after college, however, I was able to attend a World Youth Day. And there I made my first serious confession. This was a major step in bringing about a conversion in my life, but I still had a long way to go.

I started to date a girl who had been a close friend for several months. One night, as I walked her to her car, she turned around and kissed me. From there things went downhill. Even though we tried to focus on the other aspects that drew us together and on developing our friendship, we continued to have more and more physical affection. Soon it moved into passionate kissing and then petting.

We both knew something was wrong, but I wasn't strong enough to do anything about it. She was stronger than I, and she ended the relationship.

To help me heal from the brokenness I felt, a friend gave me the book *I Kissed Dating Goodbye* by Joshua Harris. Harris may not be Catholic, but the book taught me how to properly see a woman as something other than an object for my pleasure. It also stoked the fires of my desire to be a better man and learn what real love is. I read more and more about the godly way to have relationships. Eventually I started learning about the Church and her teachings, thanks to the many good Catholic materials available.

I began to go to confession often and to pray a daily rosary. I know Our Lady was instrumental in healing my vision of women. Through her prayers I was able to stop viewing pornography and masturbating.

Then I discovered John Paul II's theology of the body. It was exactly what I had been looking for and needed! It gave me a new understanding of the Church's teaching on human sexuality and helped me understand how sex is a beautiful expression of love. I became extremely passionate about Catholic manhood, Natural Family Planning, the sacraments, and true love. I started to share the pope's message with friends.

I was asked to participate in a panel on the theology of the body at a local Catholic school. I spoke about modesty, a talk that I believe was perfectly suited for me because of the struggles I had. I had become very zealous about modesty in my own life—in action, speech, dress, and media—and now wanted to share about that virtue with others.

With continued study and prayer, I grew in knowledge and love of the theology of the body. I switched my field of work to theology and, by God's providence, started working as the director of religious education at an area parish. This opportunity gave me additional avenues for sharing the theology of the body.

I entered into another relationship, one that was much more mature than the previous one. We decided that it would be best to follow Joshua Harris's advice to save our first kiss for our wedding day. This was effective in deterring improper physical affection but did not completely still the desires that stirred within. I had not fully purified my love.

The two of us read about the theology of the body together and resolved to fight the physical temptations together, with God, as much as we could. Slowly but surely we learned the way to purity and chastity in our relationship. I dreamt of a future in which God would have worked through all our struggles and made us a shining example of sacrificial love to all those with whom we came into contact.

Unfortunately my girlfriend broke off our relationship. God had other plans in mind for both of us.

Grace Upon Grace

I still needed work. I needed to master my desires for physical intimacy, to be freed from the slavery of lust. I also needed a fair dose of humility and a good kick in the pants to wake up my spiritual life, which had become somewhat robotic. A relationship with God really *must* be the basis of a marriage.

I turned again to prayer, the sacraments, and the teachings of the Church, learning more and more about sacrificial love and keeping faith through dark, dry times. God has continued to work on me and is sculpting me into the man I was created to be, knocking away many of my worthless attachments to this world. I have prayed for my future wife every day and am now engaged. I also pray for the women in my previous relationships.

I continue to study John Paul II's theology of the body, and I keep learning new things. These teachings set me alive with a renewed, fervent zeal for the faith and for true, loving, Catholic manhood. I also continue to use the teachings as a tool to evangelize others. I am blessed to already see fruits from these efforts!

God has also recently provided me with an opportunity to study for and receive a master's degree in theology. My desire is to continue to learn about the teachings of John Paul II's theology of the body and to share them with as many others as I can. I am happy to have God use me as a simple instrument and example of how knowing the truth about our bodies can transform our lives.

. . . .

"No One Will Take Your Joy From You" (John 16:22)
Sr. Miriam James Heidland

When I look at the plans I had for my life, I see that I never thought of becoming a religious sister, and I never thought that God had mercy and a passionate love for me. While I was growing up, Catholicism seemed to be an enforced set of rules that I didn't understand, and I didn't think that redemption, freedom, and true love would be something that I would one day live and breathe. John Paul II's theology of the body opened the doors to more than I could imagine.

I grew up Catholic, and my family went to Mass *every* Sunday. We might be in the middle of nowhere camping, and my mom would find a Mass to attend. My brother and I thought it was lame; we didn't see why we had to go to Mass when it was so boring. CCD classes were also part of my formation, but the beautiful realities of our faith didn't penetrate my heart. Only later would I be set on fire with the healing love of Jesus.

A major area of my life that I never thought would be considered part of my faith life is my sexuality. In my family sexuality was not openly discussed, and when it was discussed, it could be summarized as "*Don't.*" Consequently sexuality didn't "go away"; it just went underground, becoming secret and shameful.

In middle school I began playing volleyball, and in high school I received a full volleyball scholarship to a Division 1 university. It was there that I thought all of my dreams would come true. I bought into the lie that I could do whatever I wanted, and it would make me happy.

I stopped going to church regularly, partied a lot, dated a football player, and played against some of the best volleyball teams in the nation. A steady diet of fashion magazines, MTV, and sin led me to believe that I had it all. I thought that if I kept up the party and hook-up lifestyle, I would be happy.

But this all came crashing down. Often, in the quiet moments of the night, after I had been out having fun, thoughts would bubble to the surface. These thoughts challenged what I believed happiness was. When I was honest with myself, I found I was empty.

As the sin deepened in my life and drinking became too regular, I would wake up in the morning not wanting to remember the night before and wishing my life was over. The world's idea of "sexual liberation" was a lie. It didn't free people; it destroyed them. I was starving for something more.

Something Better

It was through the true love of a priest that I became a religious sister.

When I was in college, I met a priest from the Society of Our Lady of the Most Holy Trinity. He was the first person in my life who could answer my deepest questions. I wanted to know, "What is the meaning of life?" "Does my little life make a difference in this grand scheme of things?" "What is my destiny?"

Father helped guide me on the path of finding what my heart was looking for. He loved me, as does Jesus, in the ugly parts of my life and in my sin, and he believed in me when I didn't believe in myself. His love inspired me to want to walk with God and become a better person. This love changed everything, and I entered formation to become a religious sister.

During my initial religious formation, I heard about John Paul II's theology of the body. I listened to a CD series and found it interesting, but since I was embarking on a life without sex, I thought it didn't really apply to me. Besides, I reasoned, I had to bury all of my hurt from the past because I was starting a new life, and those things didn't matter anymore. I was very wrong.

As I progressed in religious life, I saw that I had a lot of wounds, and I was still dealing with a tremendous amount of guilt and shame from my past. I put on a mask of perfection, because I was terrified that someone might find out what I had done and what had been done to me. I kept my emotions and desires turned off. It was easier that way; I didn't know how to integrate them into religious life.

I came across a book about the theology of the body at this time, and it brought me much hope. As healing deepened in different areas of my life, I found myself more and more hungry for the beautiful truths of the theology of the body. The more I read, studied, and prayed about the beauty of sexuality and the deep blessings of being made a woman in the image and like-ness of God, the more my life changed. This is the Good News of Christ!

Two realities in the theology of the body particularly pierced me: those of a woman as a reflection of eternal beauty and of a woman as a mystery worth pursuing. For all the "beauty" I had sought in my life, I had never considered myself a special reflection of the beauty of God. On the contrary, society seemed to be telling me to dislike my looks.

Women buy products to achieve fleeting beauty. Plastic surgery is a fifteen-billion-dollar business and is becoming a norm in many social circles. But for all of this emphasis on Barbie-doll beauty, it seems that fewer and fewer women are truly happy with themselves.

We all know we are made for more and called to more than a superficial, changing standard of beauty. We all yearn to be truly beautiful and be found truly beautiful.

John Paul II's theology of the body taught me that I am beautiful in my very *essence*. God blessed women with a particular, powerful gift to lead others to him and to be a very reflection of his endless beauty. I had never read anything like this in any fashion magazine or seen it on any TV show. It was refreshing and rang true with me.

Another lie that society tells women is that we have to let it all hang out to be considered attractive. There is no mystery left in most of the clothing for sale, and modesty is often synonymous with ugliness. This is a great misfortune for women and men.

Why do people find the Mona Lisa so enchanting? Perhaps because she hides within her wry smile a deep mystery. Women are mysterious; God has made us so.

Within every woman is a "garden enclosed," which deserves to be protected and preserved for only the Bridegroom. Women are warriors for life, and we stand up for the individual person who is threatened. But there is something tender and hidden within a woman, and the noble find the mystery of who she is worthy of pursuit. She in turn reveals herself to the noble bridegroom, the one who is worthy. Jason Evert writes that women are "masters of their own mystery."[1] We cannot be coerced or manipulated to reveal ourselves; this would be a mockery of the gift.

This has shed a whole new light for me on the meaning of being a spouse of Christ for all eternity. To realize that Jesus seeks to enter ever more deeply into my heart is a great joy. His noble pursuit of me and my heart allows me to open myself in ways I never thought possible. His healing touch is gentle. The theology of the body has enriched my religious life a hundredfold.

We are reflections of the mystery of God. God, who is all beautiful and true but who does not throw himself at us, reveals himself to us as we seek him with pure motives. To the one who seeks ardently and rightly, God reveals his very heart.

The Mystery Lived

These truths continue to make their way into hidden paths of my heart. I learn new things about myself every day. Sometimes these truths bring me joy, sometimes they bring me tears, but there is always more. Every day I walk this journey with Jesus; I have a living encounter with Love himself.

I know now that the story of my life does not end with suffering and sorrow. Death does not have the last word. Christ came to truly redeem me and reclaim me for himself. I have tasted this redemption, and I have seen. I believe.

When I look at the brokenness of my past and the residue I deal with today, I am absolutely and completely convinced that the teaching of the theology of the body is for this time in history, and it will heal the world. Everyone holds within the hunger for satisfaction, beauty, meaning, and love. The world has fed us lies and bitterness, and many people are crying out for the truth, the truth that eternally satisfies. There is healing, redemption, and love no matter what the wound.

I am deeply grateful to John Paul II for having the courage to write something as transformative as the theology of the body, for reminding us who we are and of the great dignity to which we are called. He truly is a father to the world, not allowing us to wallow in the mud but inviting us to feast at the banquet of God's table in heaven, where we all belong. I am also grateful to people who tirelessly spread this message and, more importantly, strive to live it in their daily lives.

John Paul II said, "Dear young people, the Church needs genuine witnesses for the new evangelization: men and women whose lives have been transformed by meeting with Jesus."[2]

Let us set the world on fire.

. . . .

Sr. Miriam James Heidland is a member of the Society of Our Lady of the Most Holy Trinity (SOLT). She serves as a director of the apostolic novitiate.

. . . .

.

BURIED TREASURE

Jonathan

I am currently in the seminary because of John Paul II's theology of the body. The powerful teachings about life, the incarnate love of God through Jesus Christ, and our call to reflect divine love throughout every part of our lives have allowed me to hear God and receive an encouraging nudge in my journey of faith. The pope's unique insights on celibacy and divine love changed my vision of the priesthood. And now I am discovering the image of Christ lived out in my own life.

The Search

After college I was a bewildered young man absorbed in a fantasy of materialism and romantic affection. Full of worldly ambition, I went from city to city in pursuit of an illustrious career and a passionate love life. I found myself in the big-city party scene, where I became utterly disenchanted. I was hungry for new ideas and sure convictions. I was hungry for truth.

On one particular Tuesday morning, just days before I was slated to receive a promotion at work, I looked my boss in the eye and calmly declared, "This isn't for me." Then I shook my surprised coworkers' hands and walked out of the office, with no idea how I was going to pay my rent or the loan on my new car. Yet somewhere inside I felt I was doing the right thing.

Later that night, in a state of some anxiety, I picked up a small prayer book and skimmed until a quote caught my eye: "[M]an, who is the only creature on earth which God willed for itself, cannot fully find himself except through a sincere gift of himself."[1]

This quote from Vatican II, one that John Paul II frequently referenced, was my first encounter with the pope's theology of the body. I truly believe that John Paul II was with me that night, to intercede on my behalf in order to encourage me to go deeper within. God was pushing me to discover my individual self and explore my vocation in Christ.

The following day I drove seven hours to visit my mother. As I walked in the door, I noticed an old church bulletin lying face-down on her coffee table. When I sat down, an announcement petitioning for yearlong missionary workers in Mexico caught my eye. I knew this was the first step toward answering the call of God.

It took about a week to complete the application process and another week to sell my car and muster the willpower to part ways with my lovely girlfriend. Three weeks after walking out of the office and leaving my former way of life, I was on my way to the home of the Virgin of Guadalupe. I would work as a full-time volunteer at a children's home run by a religious order of sisters.

Not long after I settled into my small and dirty new home in Queretaro, Mexico, I began to pray with the seven nuns who managed the house of sixty-plus abandoned children. Since my Spanish was basic, I could only pray alongside them in spirit at first. In their modest chapel hung a unique picture of Pope John Paul II, holding his arms out and smiling as if embracing us as we prayed. To this day that image comes to me in moments of silence when I am feeling lonely at seminary.

Sometime during the first few months in Mexico, the idea of seminary resonated in the back of my mind. But to become a lifelong celibate priest was a foreign and unnatural idea to me. What a concept—to deny the desires of the body! Since grade school I had focused much of my attention on chasing girls, and I still loved the idea of pursuing women.

Eureka!

Then one day, while going through a give-away box, I uncovered a buried treasure that transformed my thinking forever. It was a book on John Paul II's theology of the body. I plowed through the entire volume in three days, experiencing many *eureka* moments that still echo in my mind and seep into my conversations today.

I learned that rather than trying to ignore lust or trying to use my own willpower to overcome it, I must constantly let go of my misdirected desires, give them to Christ in prayer, and faithfully allow him to correct them. This idea revolutionized my approach to self-discipline and gave me a healthier perspective on God's gift of sexuality.

As I reflected on these explanations of John Paul II's original catechesis, I ultimately came to believe that celibacy for the kingdom is an effective sign that the body, whose final end is not the grave but rather heaven, is directed to glorification with Jesus Christ. Instead of understanding celibacy as an impossible undertaking, I began to think of it as a real opportunity that I might have now in this life to grow closer to Jesus. I started to see and comprehend a new reality called "the heavenly marriage."

If I were to live celibacy as a priest, I had to learn to love others through my celibacy, not despite it. I could step outside of time and space and proclaim to the world that God's kingdom had come and that I was a participant in the heavenly marriage between Christ and his Church.

I began to build my self-discipline and to seek a better understanding of my sexuality. It felt as if someone had plugged me into a light socket. I began to see myself as a brother to Christ, and I was able to connect with the children and nuns on a deeper level than before. I became a gift to them, and they became a gift to me. Together the nuns and I worked to care for the children out of a pure and honest love, a love much greater than anything of this natural world.

The priesthood began to make sense to me. The very thoughts of celibacy and the simple life became beautiful revolutions in my mind. I applied to seminary and started memorizing Latin hymns and participating in Morning Prayer at 6 AM every day in the chapel. My decision to pursue the priesthood felt very risky, but I knew that God had his plan for my life written already. It is my job to try and understand and then live that plan out.

Coming Home

My first semester in seminary was arduous. I came back to the United States to study, and that was a shock to my system. I had grown accustomed to the very simple, serene, and minimalistic life in Mexico.

Also I was captivated by some correspondence with my former girlfriend. Although we had remained friends in a theoretical sense, we hadn't spoken since before my yearlong stay in Mexico. It was surprising how much a few sweet words in a lonely moment could shake up my being.

With just a morsel of this all-too-familiar way of life, somewhere inside I began to feel the inconvenient pull back to Christ's love that John Paul II had introduced me to in Mexico. Through spiritual direction, Christ reminded me that there was a better life for me, free of self-delusion and emotional confusion.

It was time to let go of my old self. This was very difficult, and it is something that continues to happen every day.

As I wander more deeply into the mysteries of the Church, guided by the teachings of John Paul II's theology of the body, I am gradually becoming more aware of the transforming power of the cross. It is a thorny and strenuous journey at times but one that can be completed. Through daily commitment and being close to the Eucharist, I have developed new convictions that can make a unique impact for Christ.

With great hope John Paul II proclaims that just as much as our bodily desires enslave us by disordering our passions, so does the power of the cross free us to be gifts to others. Now celibacy points me to the ultimate purpose and meaning of my sexuality, eternal union with Christ.

. . . .

WHAT DIFFERENCE DOES IT MAKE?
Patty Schneier

On October 26, 2003, in Vandalia, Illinois, I nervously spoke these words in front of approximately five hundred people: "My name is Patty Schneier. The first thing I must tell all of you—up-front—is that I am not a theologian, I am not a scholar, and I have never written a book. I am an ordinary housewife, and I have never done any public speaking in my life."

With these words a new ministry was born, and my hidden days as an ordinary housewife were changed forever. Yes, I'm still the parent volunteer and carpooling soccer mom who cantors at Sunday Mass, loves to entertain, and longs for free time to work on her scrapbook. But intermingled between baseball tournaments, orthodontist appointments, and piano lessons are my travels across the United States and Canada, speaking at parishes, schools, and Catholic conferences. I speak to bishops and priests, teachers and parents, women of all ages—even women in prison. Wherever I go I bring the good news of the theology of the body.

I witness the hunger for truth in the hearts of thousands upon thousands. The young, old, rich, and poor have shared with me their stories of pain and heartbreak, misery and suffering, due to the misuse and misunderstanding of human sexuality. Yet I also see the beautiful tears of repentance and hope in the eyes of those who want something more. They want authentic love.

It is a privilege and a joy to be a part of the theology of the body revolution that is taking root in our culture. But I never, in my wildest dreams, thought I would be involved in this work. In fact, I still say, "Pinch me," whenever I am asked to go to a new city, give a keynote address, or be a guest on Catholic radio.

Indeed, my whole world has changed because of the theology of the body. But far greater than any new talks, new articles, or changes in my daily schedule, the real transformation occurred in the secret, private recesses of my heart—and in my husband's heart as well.

God Speaks; We Listen

On January 7, 2002, the Sisters of the Apostles of the Interior Life began a weeklong mission at St. Ferdinand Church in Florissant, Missouri. My husband, Larry, and I, active members of our parish community, attended every evening. The sisters inspired me to search for holiness by following the daily readings of the Church each morning and reflecting in my prayer journal.

What began as simply a great new way to start my day became extremely difficult when I was confronted with 1 John 5:3: "For this is the love of God, that we keep his commandments. And his commandments are not burdensome."

His commandments are not *burdensome*? "Give me a break," I thought. I could immediately think of an area that proved this Scripture verse to be false—namely, the Catholic Church's teachings on sex and marriage. I knew this was a huge burden to me and millions of contracepting Catholics worldwide. So I issued my challenge to God: "If your word is truth, prove it. Prove that it isn't a burden to follow the Church's teachings on sex and marriage."

I asked in arrogance; God answered in love and mercy. The Scripture readings suddenly seemed to speak to me personally day after day. God didn't let up, and he didn't let me go, though I wrestled with him. I argued that contraception was no big deal, that it was simply a side issue. What difference did it really make?

Eventually a dear friend gave me the book *Good News About Sex & Marriage: Answers to Your Honest Questions About Catholic Teaching* by Christopher West. It pierced right through my hardened heart, leaving me speechless and sobbing. I wanted the kind of marriage described in the book. I wanted to love and be loved by my husband in this way. Finally, for the first time in my life, I recognized contraception for what it really was—a counterfeit.

On January 25, 2002, I received the sacrament of reconciliation, and I asked Larry to read Christopher West's book, as a favor to me. Within twenty-four hours he finished the book, called up our pastor, and received the sacrament of reconciliation as well. That night we threw out the contraceptives. This was *the* defining moment in our marriage.

As we look back now, that initial conversion was only the tip of the iceberg. We couldn't get enough of the theology of the body. We read books on it, listened to CDs, and attended seminars at every opportunity. We took a class on Natural Family Planning, and I switched to an NFP-only OB-GYN. We also started connecting with other families for moral support.

Now What?

Most importantly we began praying together as a couple, trying to figure out, "How are we going to *live* this? How are we going to love, day in and day out, in light of this newfound truth?"

Everything in our thirteen-year marriage had to be reevaluated. The words *free*, *faithful*, *total*, and *fruitful* became the focus of long, late-night discussions, which guided us closer to the light. We wanted to be sincere gifts to each other, but in order to do so, we had to confront many counterfeits, temptations, and habits. Every touch, every physical action, every sexual act, became an opportunity to grow and learn how to truly love.

It was painful to peel through layer after layer and recognize the assumptions, attitudes, and distortions that had crept into our thinking. How many times had I used sex as a reward, withheld my love as a punishment, or simply given in to appease my husband? How many times had I felt obligated or manipulated to act a certain way, dress a certain way, talk a certain way? How many times did I sense my husband's ulterior motive when he asked if I wanted a back rub?

Suddenly these counterfeits had no place in our marriage, for they were distortions of freely given love. Anything that could not stand up to the words *free*, *faithful*, *total*, and *fruitful*, we no longer desired. With each new step forward, we turned the corner to a different area, however, that needed adjustment.

When we first analyzed the faithfulness of our marriage, we thought, "No problem here. We've been faithful to each other for thirteen years." Deeper reflection, however, helped us understand that every act of intercourse is meant to "speak" the language of our marriage vows—that we are physically renewing our sacred covenant and pledging our lifelong fidelity in the marital embrace. I was shocked beyond belief, because that particular thought had never occurred to me. *A renewal of marriage vows?* That was *not* going on in my bedroom. And yet I wanted this renewal of vows. I wanted to be transported in time and place to the altar of our vows and our wedding night.

And so we began to speak our vows to each other, over and over again, in our words and our actions. The meaning of our sexual union completely changed.

A Total Gift of Self

Total was, no doubt, the word that sparked our initial conversion and led us to eliminate all forms of contraception. We could easily see that contraception destroyed the possibility of a total gift of self. We had indeed withheld our fertility, the core of our being, from each other. But there was far more to it—especially for me.

I had many underlying hang-ups about my body. I hated my thunder thighs, flabby arms, big back porch, varicose veins, and so on. Because of this I found it difficult to delight in the human body or to receive the gift of touch. I had to learn to give my entire body to my husband and receive the gift of his body as well.

Many women struggle in this area, and I can only testify that my transformation came about because of the changes in Larry. He was serious about loving me freely, faithfully, totally, and fruitfully—and doing whatever it took to live it. His mission became to love me as Christ loved the Church, with life-giving service and sacrifice.

Larry fasted and prayed. He would ask, "How can I best love you tonight?" How he loved me was so beautiful that it freed me to respond with passion and delight. I became free to accept my body, receive his body, and truly desire the total gift of self.

This was an unexpected surprise for both of us. Who would have thought that the woman who frequently claimed "headache" was now head over heels in love with her husband and couldn't wait to express this love? So often Larry would comment, "If other guys only knew. If they only knew."

We marveled at the effects the theology of the body was having on our sex life and our entire marriage: Our vocabulary changed, our parenting changed, and our appreciation of the Catholic faith changed. We could no longer fathom life as before. Our hearts longed to incorporate this new discovery into every aspect of our lives. This, however, proved easier said than done.

The challenge came back to the area of fruitfulness. Fears, doubts, and questions surfaced. Were we truly open to new life? Did we desire our marriage to be both unitive and procreative? Could we trust like never before and say, "Thy will be done," with every act of intercourse?

Slowly but surely we experienced firsthand that true love casts out all fear (see 1 John 4:18). After much soul-searching and prayer, it came down to surrender and trust—surrendering our entire lives to each other and to God, and then trusting in his perfect plan for our future. We continue to pray that every act of love will bear great fruit for our marriage and for the kingdom of God, and then we allow God to choose the fruit.

The irony of our journey is that for many years when we were physically fertile, we feared any possible fruit and desired barrenness. Now, in our physical barrenness, we desire fruitfulness. For many outsiders looking in, our story seems incomplete. I have received anonymous letters, personal attacks, and questions from inquiring minds: "Well, where's the fruit? Why haven't you had another baby?"

With public ministry, unfortunately, comes public scrutiny. I have had to learn how to respond to such questions without divulging all the details of my personal medical history. God has opened many new doors for us, but he has also shut doors.

Our journey has included anticipation and joy beyond our wildest imagination, spiritual fruit, and the fruits of a new ministry. Countless people have entered our lives, and their conversions encourage and inspire us daily. We see the "fruit" of God all around us.

Years have passed since our conversion in 2002, but January 25 remains for us a special anniversary date, when we celebrate what God has done in our lives through the theology of the body: What was once weakness is now strength; selfishness has been replaced with sacrifice; dissent has been transformed into faith. Our respect for each other has skyrocketed, and we have experienced unity in our marriage like never before.

At the same time we realize we have only begun to scratch the surface of this deep treasure. And so we continue to reflect, learn, and study the theology of the body, in order to let it sink more deeply into our hearts and then share it with the world. We are forever grateful!

. . . .

Patty Schneier is a lifelong Catholic, a housewife, and a mother of three from the archdiocese of St. Louis. She shares the good news about love and life at parishes and Catholic conferences throughout the country. To learn more about her ministry, visit www.pattyschneier.com.

. . . .

C H A P T E R | **T** **E** **N**

Two Women, One Lord, One Truth, One Way
Trey Cashion

The essence of Pope John Paul II's theology of the body is summed up in the following words: The body, and it alone, is capable of making the invisible—the spiritual and the divine—visible. Until one experiences this truth concretely, it seems more of a philosophical catchphrase than a truth on which to base one's life. Moreover, discussions of the pope's theology of the body are often limited to issues of human sexuality. This makes sense because sexuality is the focus of this study of God through the human body, particularly within the context of being man and woman.

However, this gift of God to the Church through John Paul II has much broader application to our bodily lives. Vatican II states, "One of the gravest errors of our time is the dichotomy between the faith which many profess and the practice of their daily lives."[1] Our faith and our lives should be an integrated whole. In other words, what we believe about God, man, the meaning of life, and so on should take concrete form in what we do day to day. Faith and life belong together.

In fact, when we live this integration of faith and life, God is able to communicate his truth to a world in desperate need of it. The Word becomes incarnate through our witness.

I came to understand the truth about love in an incarnate way through two women in my life—one through her passion and death, the other through her welcoming of new life. These happen to be the two women I have loved the most, my mother and my wife. My mother said yes to her death; my wife said yes to triplets. Both of them made love and faith concrete for me. They put flesh, a body, on the concept. They made the invisible visible.

The Incarnation of Love

When Mom was diagnosed with cancer, she was adamant about not being put in a hospital bed. Because of the size of the tumor in her pancreas, she had to sleep sitting up. My dad purchased a two-seat recliner so that they could still sleep next to each other. Dad could recline all the way back while Mom slept sitting up right next to him.

They had done this for about a month when I received a phone call from Dad, early on the morning of December 14, 1998. Mom had been up all night, and the morphine was not able to keep her from agonizing pain. Dad said that today might be the day. So I got up and headed to my parents' house.

I stopped by the church to pray for Mom. As I picked up the missalette to find the readings of the day, I noticed that it was the feast day of St. John of the Cross—a realization that gained meaning as the day progressed.

I left the church, hoping that my stop didn't mean missing the opportunity to say good-bye to Mom. Upon my arrival I was amazed to see that she was not in pain and seemed to be in good spirits. In fact, she was doing so well that we told my brother he could finish his finals at dental school and then come home. It looked as if the danger had passed.

Later the hospice physician arrived and suggested again that Mom consider a hospital bed. After a momentary silence she looked up and said, "I think that would be fine." We all were surprised.

The bed was ordered, and it arrived early in the afternoon. While it was being set up, we talked with Mom, who remained in good spirits. It was amazing—miraculous, it seemed.

Once the bed was ready, Dad and I helped Mom get out of the chair and onto the new bed. As she lay down she immediately writhed in pain. We tried morphine. We tried adjusting the bed. Nothing alleviated the pain. It was horrible. It was constant. All we could do was pray the rosary and allow Mom to squeeze our hands.

An hour passed and then another. As the end of the third hour approached, I couldn't take it any more. I went into the next room and opened my Bible to the Crucifixion scene of Matthew's Gospel. I remember crying out, "Lord, do something. You were on the cross for only three hours. This is horrible. Please do something."

There was a knock on the door. I opened it, and there was my cousin saying, "She's gone." I went to Mom's new bed. I looked up at the clock. It was just past 6:00 PM. She had been on the hospital bed for three hours.

God made the Crucifixion of Christ concrete for my family. I had helped to place Mom on her cross, the hospital bed, just as my sins helped place Christ on his cross. She had said yes to God's plan, just as Christ had said yes. In her body Mom was transformed into the image of her Savior. In her body the invisible became visible.

Multiplying the Incarnation

In a completely different manner, my wife's *yes* accomplished the same end: God made himself present through her body.

In about the twelfth week of her pregnancy, we found out that Stephanie was measuring three weeks larger than she was supposed to. The doctor scheduled a sonogram to see if she might be pregnant with twins. Seven years earlier we had been told we might not be able to have children. We then had three children in just over four years, and now we might be having twins. The thought was daunting.

Stephanie and I talked the night before the sonogram. We joked that God had allowed this in order to show us that he is in control and we are not. He was putting us in a situation that we knew we couldn't handle.

The next day I got up and went to work. I would meet Stephanie at the doctor's office later, so I could help with the kids and find out whether twins were on the way.

When I arrived at the office, Stephanie was already in the examination room. She told me that she had been in such a hurry that she forgot to pray before they left the house. So in the parking lot, she prayed with the kids using Mary's answer to Gabriel at the Annunciation: "Let it be to me according to your word" (Luke 1:37). It was a perfect prayer—a *yes* to God's plan.

The doctor walked in and began the sonogram. It sure looked as if there was more than one child. The doctor didn't say anything. After scanning for some time, he stopped and said that we were having twins. He looked at Stephanie and then at me before he noticed the three children standing behind me—a five-year-old, a four-year-old, and a two-year-old. His face turned the color of his coat. He swallowed, regained his composure, and then began to discuss what we could expect.

Then he stopped and said, "You know, I missed diagnosing triplets recently. Let me take another look just to make sure." He looked once. He looked twice without saying anything. The third time he looked at my wife and said, "There are three in there. You're having triplets."

Again he looked at me and at the three children behind me. The whiteness returned to his face as he lowered his head and said to my wife, "What are you going to do?"

Stephanie smiled and calmly said, "I hope we're going to have three healthy babies." That was the first of many *yeses* from my wife.

Fruitful Sacrifice

We began seeing a doctor who specializes in multiple births. She told us we would be lucky to get the pregnancy to thirty weeks, given the fact that we had three little ones at home. My wife asked her what would be the longest time she would let a triplet pregnancy continue. The doctor said thirty-six weeks. My wife looked at her and with great confidence said, "Well, we'll be praying for thirty-six weeks then."

The doctor chuckled and said, "Let's just hope you get to thirty weeks."

To get to thirty-six weeks, we knew that some things would have to be done. First, we needed as many prayers as possible. Through friends we had multiple churches praying for the same thing: healthy triplets and thirty-six weeks. It was very specific. We had so many people praying for us that for years after the birth, people we had never met before would walk up to us at restaurants, grocery stores, and other public places and say they remembered praying for us.

Second, my wife's routine would have to change. The doctor told us our only hope was for Stephanie to spend no more than ten minutes of every hour on her feet. The rest of the time had to be spent in bed. This meant she would be unable to cook meals, wash clothes, pick up children, put children down for naps, clean the house, and so on. In other words, she would have to give up almost all she was used to doing.

Stephanie is an extraordinarily organized and capable home-maker. Everything is usually in perfect order. However, at this time in our lives, she was at the pinnacle of her orderliness. She knew how everything was supposed to be—when children went down for naps, which clothes could and could not be washed with other clothes, how to get the kids to play together happily, and so on. She also knew how she liked things—where decorations went on tables, how clean the floor needed to be, and more. All this would be left in my hands (and the hands of many self-less volunteer helpers) if we were going to try to get to thirty-six weeks.

This was another cross in our family. Stephanie would have to observe my ineptitude at handling the children in the morning. She would have to see the results of colors and whites being washed together. She would have to allow others to clean and arrange the house in ways different from her own. She would have to allow others to pick up and comfort her babies when they fell and scraped their knees.

If the triplets were going to have the best opportunity to live, Stephanie would have to die to all of this. She had to die to herself. And she would have to do this for three to four months in her own home.

And that is exactly what she did. I do not remember her ever complaining about my ineptitude in the laundry room or with the children. She always encouraged me and even made us laugh. She kept me going. She brought me life in her dying to herself. She showed me love incarnate. For almost four months she cheerfully embraced her cross for the sake of her children (both inside and outside of the womb) and for her spouse. She made Christ visible in and through her body.

After four months of bed rest, on May 9, 2001, at thirty-five weeks and five days, three healthy triplets were born—Trenton Kolbe, Kennedy Ambrose, and Kingsley Kay. The hospital—one that specializes in high-risk pregnancies—had never seen anything like it. All three went to a level-2 nursery rather than a level 3 (for very sick newborns). All three were discharged on the same day—something that had never happened before at this hospital. All three spent less than two weeks in the hospital—which had rarely happened with triplets.

Today the triplets are normal eight-year-olds because of the prayers of many people. And because my wife died so that they might live.

My mother and my wife made the theology of the body real for me. They allowed the Incarnation to come alive through their sacrifices. In them I have seen faith and life integrated. In them I have seen Christ.

We all have opportunities to make the invisible God visible to others. In so doing we evangelize in and through our circumstances, in our day-to-day lives. We bring Christ alive for others.

. . . .

Trey and Stephanie Cashion are parents to six children. Trey, the founder of MysteryofParenthood.com and FamilyWay.org, is a popular speaker on the practical application of Church teaching to everyday life. He coauthored Together in God's Image, *a marriage preparation program. To learn more about his ministry, visit tmgspeakers.com or MysteryofParenthood.com.*

. . . .

TAKEN BY LOVE
Stephanie Balser

My story may not sound radical to the world, because it is not one of an extreme conversion. I am an average twenty-one-year-old woman. But there is one way in which I am not average: I've come to know God's personal and intimate love for me, and I experience it on a daily basis.

My story is a love story between myself and my God. It's the story of how he has slowly but surely captivated my heart, transformed my life, and molded me into the woman I am today. But it has been a journey, and it is largely Pope John Paul II's theology of the body that has opened my eyes to the truth of God's love.

Virtue and Vice

I'm a cradle Catholic, and I grew up in a great family, which consisted of my mom, dad, brother, sister, and myself. I went to Catholic schools for ten years, then ventured into the realm of public high school. Upon beginning my freshman year, I was a modest female adolescent; my values had been well instilled by my family and the Church.

But as a young teenager in a new place, I wanted badly to be noticed. I longed to stand out in some way. And right away I had my eye on a particular guy who was a star player of the football team (we can call him "Steven"). I instinctively made it my goal to show Steven I was good enough for him.

At first we developed a genuine friendship: I offered Steven my "inner" beauty. I was kind, compassionate, and always there for him when he needed something. But after a while it seemed as if that wasn't enough. He was losing interest, and I was desperate to keep his attention. So I began to offer him my outer beauty.

I started to dress immodestly and act differently. I wanted to be irresistible. After two years I finally "got" Steven. We started dating the fall of my junior year.

I was ecstatic. This was my biggest accomplishment. I had proven to myself I could get anybody; it was just a matter of how much I had to give away.

I enjoyed the attention and affection I was receiving and wanted to continue to impress Steven so I wouldn't lose hold of him. My values, to which I had held fast my entire life, began to crumble. I kept telling myself, "If this is OK, what's a little bit more?" I was naive, and my boyfriend introduced me to a whole new world of experiences. Many of the choices we made indicated values far from the ones I had held.

I dated Steven for almost two years, and the entire time I experienced inner conflict. I felt guilty but didn't do anything about it. Occasionally I would have a conversation with Steven about how I didn't feel right about the things we did. We would stop for a while but fall back into the same old routine.

I remember arguing with priests in the confessional because I didn't understand *why* what I was doing was wrong. After all,

I loved Steven. It seemed as if none of them could provide an answer I was capable of comprehending. So I continued to give myself away physically in order to fulfill my emotional needs of being desired, good enough, and loved. I wasn't satisfied, but what else was there?

The Love of My Life

By the time I got to college, the tension was building in my heart. I was tired of the way I was being treated, and I knew I deserved something better. I became involved with St. Mary's Catholic Center at Texas A&M, where I realized that there was more out there, and I wanted it.

After praying about the situation, I came to the conclusion that I needed to end my relationship with Steven. The breakup was difficult, but I recognized that God was calling me to experience something greater, and this excited me. In the following weeks I felt a great sense of freedom. I was so overwhelmed with this newfound joy that I quickly moved on from my relationship with Steven. I invested myself even more in St. Mary's and the friendships I was forming there.

Freshman year ended, summer came and went, and before long I was back at school for my sophomore year. I was getting more enthusiastic about my faith, and I wanted to go deeper. I was trying to absorb everything I was learning at school and at church.

Then one evening at Mass, the homily was about letting go of whatever prevents you from loving. At the moment those words left the priest's mouth, something struck a painful chord in my heart, and there was a deep aching within me. For the rest of Mass, I desperately tried to hold back the river of tears that was welling up. As soon as Mass was over, I ran out of church. I ran all the way back to my dorm room, got in my car, and drove to a place where I knew I could be alone with God.

While driving my heart broke open, and I cried the hardest I've ever cried in my entire life. I was aware that God was about to enter my life deeply, and the knowledge of everything that was going on in my heart came flooding into my consciousness at once. I sincerely desired to love God more, I longed to give him all of myself, I wanted to love others more, but I couldn't. I had hit a roadblock. I was stuck, because I didn't know how to love.

I didn't even know what love truly was, nor was I sure I wanted anything to do with it. Apart from my family and friends, Steven was the only experience of "love" I had had, and if that's what love was, then I desired no part of it.

At this point I recognized that, although I had gotten over Steven quickly, I had never taken the time to heal from the relationship, and it had affected me in more ways than I had thought. It had distorted my view of love. Our relationship had been controlling, jealous, and completely selfish—basically, get as much as you can from the other person. And because we said, "I love you," love became these things.

I felt lost and didn't know where to turn. All I could do was trust that God would show me the way.

The Truth About Love

That first semester of my sophomore year was rough. Every day I dealt with painful, resurfacing memories. I began to understand how much I had been hurt and how much I had hurt others in my relationship with Steven.

At the same time I was allowing God to bring healing and new hope to my heart as he tenderly spoke his love to me. I frequented the sacraments of confession and the Eucharist. I tried my best to soak in God's mercy and spent a lot of time in prayer. God also put many people in my life to support me during this time of growth.

It was over Christmas break that I picked up a book that summarized John Paul II's theology of the body. I was at a bookstore, and I bought some coffee and sat down to read. Little did I know that the truth unveiled in the book would change my life.

I was fascinated, and within minutes I was hooked; this book held the answers to questions I had been wondering about—questions about love, sex, desire, and God. I began to see the meaning of life and the meaning of my body. I couldn't get enough. I felt as if I had discovered a gold mine of truth, and I thirsted for more.

As I have studied the theology of the body, prayed with it, and experienced it over the past two years, God has begun to redeem parts of my life that were lost to sin and the ways of the world. Everything has started to make sense, and I have fallen head over heals for my God.

The theology of the body has opened my eyes to the reality of *what* love is and the secret of *how* to love. The Trinity has largely revealed this to me.

Love is a total and complete gift of self: It means choosing what is best for another regardless of the cost to yourself. Participating in love encompasses two things: selfless giving and selfless receiving. I have learned that giving love is impossible if you have not first received it from the source of love. "We love, because he first loved us" (1 John 4:19).

I have perceived another key element of love: There is no grasping. Our relationship with God teaches us this. We have no need to grasp at God's love, because he already desires to give it completely to us. All we have to do is open our hearts and receive the gift. Then, in response, we offer ourselves back to him. In the same way we are called to give of ourselves to others and openly receive (not grasp at) the love another desires to give us in return.

This is where Steven and I had made a crucial mistake. We constantly grasped at each other's love. I was robbed of my gift and had nothing left to give of my own accord, which left me feeling violated, empty, and useless. Now, as I learned how to love as God loves, every relationship in my life changed. I came to understand the importance of the gift.

Who Am I?

Recently my psychology professor wrote the words "I am…" on the board and asked us to fill in the blank. My response came quite easily: I am Catholic, I am a woman, and I am loved. I can proudly say that these three things define who I am; they make up my identity. And the theology of the body helped me figure this out.

I am Catholic. The theology of the body has helped me realize the significance of the faith I have practiced my whole life. The depth of Catholicism amazes me. In particular I have come to appreciate the sacraments of the Catholic Church, especially the intimacy of the Eucharist. I never experience God's love so powerfully as when I am able to become one with him physically and spiritually.

God is absolute mystery, but he has chosen to reveal himself to us in profound ways. Everything is meant to point us to God, in the Persons of the Father, Son, and Holy Spirit, and guide us into a personal relationship with him.

I am a woman. The theology of the body has helped me uncover the mystery of my own sexuality. Many of the desires within my heart are good, but I sought fulfillment of them in the wrong places. I want to be loved and to be beautiful, and I fall prey to the lies of this confusing world, this world which demands so much but leaves us feeling worthless. I needed someone who could lead me to the truth.

The theology of the body has shed light on a woman who embodies femininity in its fullest: Mary! Over the past few years I have developed a deep love and respect for the Mother of God, and she has become my role model. Mary shows me how to be receptive and open to God's love, allowing it to transform my heart and empowering me to share this love with others.

Mary teaches me how to be beautiful, for true beauty is a mystery that must be unveiled, which is why purity is an art for the woman. Our bodies speak a love language, and we must not "throw our pearls before swine" (Matthew 7:6). I want to strive for modesty and purity in my relationships, because I can see my inherent dignity and the respect I deserve.

Most importantly, I have come to know Mary as my mom. In this mess of a world, where the reality of love and beauty has been largely distorted, she protects and guides me along the path of holiness straight to my Savior.

I am loved. Through the theology of the body, I have encountered God's amazing love for me as his daughter and beloved. Jesus' humanity makes this love all the more real and relatable. God has a personal, unique, and intimate love for me. I am a precious treasure in his eyes: He desires to be with me, he sees my beauty, and he delights in me.

I have learned that my worth does not depend on what a man, the media, my friends, or even my family tells me. My worth is found in God, and it is abundant. Knowing how much my God loves me gives me my joy, and no one can take that away from me.

The theology of the body has guided me in discovering God's special plan for me. I am loved, and I was created for love—to participate intimately in it. Most specifically God has showed me, through quite a journey, that I am called to marriage, and I couldn't be more excited.

I used to think marriage was the default option: If you weren't going to be a priest or nun, you would get married. This is absolutely false. I desire to be a wife and mother. I want to be a gift to my husband one day. I long to know Christ, love him, and give myself to him through my spouse. I want to grow in holiness with the man I marry. This is what God has created my heart for.

I have also recognized that spreading the theology of the body is part of what God is calling me to do with the rest of my life. My heart surges every time I read about it, speak about it, pray about it, or do anything related to the theology of the body.

My passion lies with young people: Teens and preteens are those I want to reach. Now that I understand why the things I did in high school were wrong, I want to bring the truth to others. I want to provide more than just, "Don't do this, and don't do that." I want to tell young people *why*, with life-giving truth that makes sense!

I am grateful to Pope John Paul II for his openness to God's grace and willingness to share himself with the world. The theology of the body has enlightened me to what love is, who I am, and what God is calling me to. Through this teaching I have discovered the only love that can truly satisfy my heart, and I have been taken by it.

My Prayer to John Paul II

Most holy Pope John Paul the Great,

I humbly ask for your intercession.

Thank you for your gift of self to this world,

to Jesus through Mary.

Thank you for helping me realize the beauty of my feminine
heart

and the true dignity of my human person.

Help me to trust in Jesus every moment of every day

and always look to Mary as my ultimate example of woman-
hood and motherhood.

I pray for the grace to be open, *neqebah*,

to receive perfectly my Beloved

and all the gifts of love that he wishes to shower upon me.

I pray for my dear brothers,

that they will be formed into faithful men.

I pray for the conversion of sinners,

that hearts will be molded to that of my sweet and precious
Jesus

through the womb of his Blessed Mother,

especially by way of the healing truth unveiled in the theology
of the body,

which you so boldly proclaimed to this broken world.

I pray for wisdom and the courage to spread this good news

according to his perfect and holy will.

And humbly I beg

for Christ to have mercy on us.

Praise and glory to his name forever and ever.

Amen.

. . . .

Stephanie Balser is a graduate of Texas A&M University.

. . . .

Organizations and Their Web Sites

Christopher West, www.christopherwest.com

Family Honor, http://familyhonor.org

The Gift Foundation, http://www.giftfoundation.org

One More Soul, www.onemoresoul.com

Our Father's Will Communications, http://www.ourfatherswill-communications.com

Pontifical John Paul II Institute, http://www.johnpaulii.edu

Theology of the Body Evangelization Team (TOBET), http://www.tobet.org

Theology of the Body Institute, http://www.tobinstitute.org

Theology of the Body International Alliance (TOBIA), www.theologyofthebody.net

Women of the Third Millennium, http://wttm.org

Books

Anderson, Carl, and Jose Granados. *Called to Love: Approaching Pope John Paul II's Theology of the Body*. New York: Doubleday, 2009.

Healy, Mary. *Men and Women Are From Eden: A Study Guide for the Theology of the Body*. Cincinnati: Servant, 2005.

John Paul II. *Man and Woman He Created Them: A Theology of the Body*. Michael Waldstein, trans. Boston: Pauline, 2006.

Shivanandan, Mary. *Crossing the Threshold of Love: A New Vision of Marriage*. Washington, D.C.: Catholic University of America Press, 1999.

West, Christopher. *Good News About Sex and Marriage: Answers to Your Honest Questions about Catholic Teaching*. Ann Arbor, Mich.: Servant, 2000.

————. *The Theology of the Body Explained: A Commentary on John Paul II's* Man and Woman He Created Them. Boston: Pauline, 2007.

————. *Theology of the Body for Beginners: A Basic Introduction to John Paul II's Sexual Revolution.* West Chester, Pa.: Ascension, 2004.

Wojtyla, Karol. *Love and Responsibility.* H.T. Willetts, trans. San Francisco: Ignatius, 1993.

Introduction

1. Augustine, *Confessions*, bk. 1, chap. 1, no. 1.
2. John Paul II, General Audience of Wednesday, February 20, 1980, available at: www.vatican.va.

Chapter Five

This Is My Body: The Most Important Words in the Universe

1. John Paul II, *Man and Woman He Created Them: A Theology of the Body*, Michael Waldstein, trans. (Boston: Pauline, 2006), 103:3, General Audience of January 5, 1983, p. 533.
2. John Paul II, *Man and Woman* 48:4, General Audience of November 12, 1980, p. 320.
3. See John Paul II, *Man and Woman* 87:5, General Audience of July 28, 1982, p. 468.
4. John Paul II, *Man and Woman* 13:1, General Audience of January 2, 1980, p. 177.
5. John Paul II, *Man and Woman* 10:2, General Audience of November 21, 1979, p. 167.
6. See John Paul II, *Man and Woman* 117b:2, General Audience of July 4, 1984, p. 613.
7. John Paul II, *Man and Woman* 51:5, General Audience of December 17, 1980, p. 335.
8. John Paul II, *Man and Woman* 68:4, General Audience of December 16, 1981, p. 396. See also Pope Benedict XVI, *In the Beginning...: A Catholic Understanding of the Story of Creation and the Fall*, Boniface Ramsey, trans. (Grand Rapids: Eerdmans, 1995), pp. 72–73.

9. C.S. Lewis, *The Four Loves* (New York: Harcourt Brace, 1991), p. 72.

10. John Paul II, *Man and Woman* 117b:6, General Audience of July 4, 1984, p. 615.

11. John Paul II, *Man and Woman* 59:3, General Audience of April 8, 1981, p. 361.

Chapter Seven

"No One Will Take Your Joy From You" (John 16:22)

1. Jason Evert, *Theology of His/Her Body* (West Chester, Pa.: Ascension, 2009), p. 17.

2. John Paul II, Message to the Youth of the World, August 6, 2004, available at: www.vatican.va.

Chapter Eight

Buried Treasure

1. Vatican II, *Gaudium et Spes*, Pastoral Constitution on the Church in the Modern World, no. 22, available at: www. vatican.va.

Chapter Ten

Two Women, One Lord, One Truth, One Way

1. *Gaudium et Spes*, no. 43, in *Vatican Council II, Volume 1: The Conciliar and Post Conciliar Documents*, rev. ed., Austin Flannery, ed. (Northport, N.Y.: Costello, 1998), p. 943.

ABOUT THE AUTHOR

Marcel LeJeune is the Assistant Director of Campus Ministry at St. Mary's Catholic Center at Texas A&M University. He speaks about the theology of the body at conferences, dioceses, and parishes around the country. He and his wife, Kristy, are the parents of five children. If you are interested in writing to Marcel, would like information about his speaking engagements, or if you want to invite him to speak to your group, please visit www.TheCatholicEvangelist.com.